# layered, tattered & stitched

## A *fabric* art WORKSHOP

Ruth Rae

## NORTH LIGHT BOOKS

Cincinnati, Ohio

www.mycraftivity.com

13 12 11 10 09   5 4 3 2 1

Distributed in Canada by Fraser Direct
100 Armstrong Avenue
Georgetown, ON, Canada  L7G 5S4
Tel: (905) 877-4411

Distributed in the U.K. and Europe by David & Charles
Brunel House, Newton Abbot, Devon, TQ12 4PU, England
Tel: (+44) 1626 323200, Fax: (+44) 1626 323319
E-mail: postmaster@davidandcharles.co.uk

Distributed in Australia by Capricorn Link
P.O. Box 704, S. Windsor, NSW 2756 Australia
Tel: (02) 4577-3555

Library of Congress Cataloging-in-Publication Data
Rae, Ruth, 1966-
    Layered, tattered, and stitched : a fabric art workshop /
    Ruth Rae. -- 1st ed.
      p. cm.
    Includes index.
    ISBN 978-1-60061-188-9 (softcover : alk. paper)
1. Textile crafts. I. Title.
TT699.R33 2009
746--dc22          2009030674

## metric conversion chart

| TO CONVERT | TO | MULTIPLY BY |
| --- | --- | --- |
| Inches | Centimeters | 2.54 |
| Centimeters | Inches | 0.4 |
| Feet | Centimeters | 30.5 |
| Centimeters | Feet | 0.03 |
| Yards | Meters | 0.9 |
| Meters | Yards | 1.1 |
| Sq. Inches | Sq. Centimeters | 6.45 |
| Sq. Centimeters | Sq. Inches | 0.16 |
| Sq. Feet | Sq. Meters | 0.09 |
| Sq. Meters | Sq. Feet | 10.8 |
| Sq. Yards | Sq. Meters | 0.8 |
| Sq. Meters | Sq. Yards | 1.2 |
| Pounds | Kilograms | 0.45 |
| Kilograms | Pounds | 2.2 |
| Ounces | Grams | 28.3 |
| Grams | Ounces | 0.035 |

fw
*media*
AN IMPRINT OF F+W MEDIA, INC.
www.fwmedia.com

Editors: Tonia Davenport, Nancy Breen
Cover Designer: Julie Barnett
Designer: Marissa Bowers
Production Coordinator: Greg Nock
Photographers: Al Parrish, Christine Polomsky
Photo Stylist: Jan Nickum

# Dedication

*To my incredible mother! You established in me the strength to believe in myself no matter how hard I struggled with reading and writing due to my dyslexia. Your sustaining love, support and encouragement, combined with the endless art supplies that you bestowed upon me, gave me a light to follow along the path to my passion and creativity. For this I am eternally grateful to you!*

# Acknowledgments

Without my dear friend Kristen Robinson, the writing of this book would not have been so effortless. Kristen, your help and support are felt sincerely and to the highest degree!

Furthermore, enormous thankfulness to Brian, my devoted husband, and to my magnificent children, Sarah-Jeanne and Brian, Jr., for allowing me the space that I need to create. Thank you for wholly sustaining and understanding my soul.

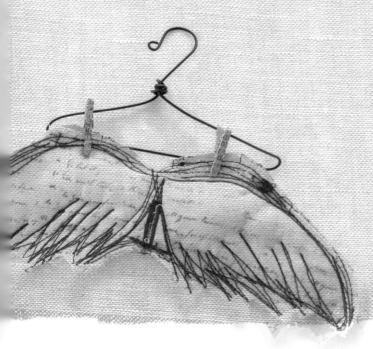

# contents

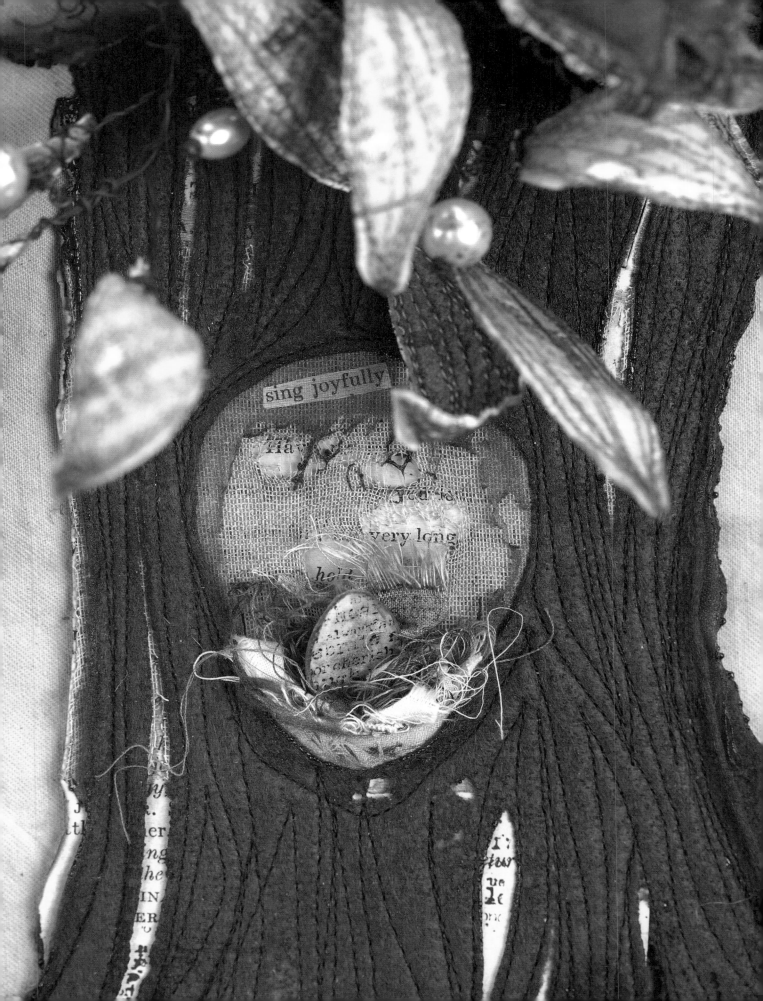

# INTRODUCTION:
# A Passion for Texture

A new trail is being blazed in fabric art. Innovative art quilters are bravely combining nontraditional elements, building on the resonance of the past while gazing toward the future of quilting. These art quilts are not intended to be useful in the same way as yesterday's quilts; they play a new artful role in warming one's soul.

When the opportunity came about to write this book, I found myself developing ideas that would join fibers, textures and techniques, weaving and intertwining them to create art. As I began the projects, I realized how much I was influenced by my work as a jeweler, merging techniques and even materials with the fabric I so enjoy as a medium.

As we build up our skills and continue to add new ones, we grow as artists, and our individual style begins to unfold before our eyes. As we develop our techniques, our intuitive color palette flows out of us while images and words we hold dear begin to resonate in our work. The process is truly an evolution within one's self.

I encourage you to imagine texture as a way of building the layers of your life. Consider thread the catalyst needed to add texture and durability to your work. Consider your sewing machine as more than a tool for creating a sound foundation; also look upon it as an art tool. Picture your thread as paint; use your hands to guide your fabric just as if the needle is your paintbrush.

Journey into the adventure of adding color to fabric with dye and paint. Deepen texture with rubber stamps and inks. Soon you will find yourself immersed, coming up with your own innovative ways of incorporating even more texture and objects into your fabric art. Once you start creating your own fabrics, you will soon find that your work truly takes on a life all its own, telling the story that you have been yearning to express in your individual art.

Through the pages of this book, you and I will explore a new realm of creativity. You'll learn the techniques that I have developed for altering and manipulating fabric to produce a time-worn appearance. Shifting new fabrics and papers generates an ancient echo that makes it seem these creations were fashioned centuries ago, yet in some way they merge what went before with the present day.

When the boundaries that many perceive in the art of sewing are eliminated, this breaking of tradition opens up a new world of textile art. I encourage you to find new ways to incorporate and combine my techniques with methods you already know and use, allowing you to grow within your own creativity. I invite you to become seduced with color and texture, and to allow your mind's eye to guide you on a creative journey through your soul.

Ruth Rae

# GATHER THESE THINGS: Tools and Supplies

These are the tools and supplies that I find indispensable in my studio. See individual projects for more about how these items are used.

## SEWING TOOLS

### Needles

I use Schmetz quilt machine needles, size 14/90, for all of my sewing needs. They have a specially tapered point designed for stitching through multiple layers.

For hand work with pearl cotton, I use size 22 tapestry needles. When I need a sharper needle, I reach for a 18/22 chenille needle.

For beading, I prefer John James #12 and #13 tapestry beading needles.

### Rotary Cutter

Combined with a good cutting mat, a rotary cutter enables you to cut free-form through many layers of fabric and papers.

### Scissors

There are several manufacturers of quality scissors, but I prefer Gingher. I find that a 12" (30cm) blade is easier on the hands. I also like to use a pair of pinking shears for decorative edges.

### Sewing Machine

In my home studio I use a Bernina Aurora 440 QE. I am also very fond of the Singer 221 Featherweight™, which I use when traveling to teach.

## FABRIC, FIBERS AND THREADS—OH, MY!

### Embroidery Thread

For hand detail work, I use DMC® Pearl Cotton #5. I also use five-ply embroidery threads but have found that the two-ply nature of the pearl cotton is less likely to knot up when stitching.

For beading, I use white Nymo thread in size B or D along with my beading needle. I apply colored marker to the thread so it will match the color of the bead.

### Felt

I adore wool felt (70 percent wool/30 percent rayon) for its amazing texture as well as the stunning range of colors available only in wool. When washed in hot water, it will pucker up and shrink about 8 percent. Wool felt does not burn, but it will blacken when exposed to a heat gun or flame. I use wool felt with Kunin craft felt when I do not want to see a reaction in a layer.

Kunin craft felt is synthetic and comes in an array of colors, and the cost is economical. When treated with a heat gun, Kunin felt buckles and shrinks, producing an amazing effect. Applying the direct flame of a tea light candle to Kunin results in a melted edge.

### Fiberfill

Fiberfill can be used to help give dimension to a piece.

### Lace and Doilies

I'm happiest when I find a piece of antique lace or a doily that is in a state of disrepair—I don't have mixed feelings about tearing it up or dyeing it! You can also use new 100 percent cotton lace.

### Muslin

Buy bleached and unbleached muslin by the bolt.

### Organza

I use synthetic organza for its sheerness as well as its ability to house objects in sewn works. Organza burns amazingly well, so you can alter it slightly with a tea light candle or change it dramatically with a heat gun.

### Printable Fabric Sheets

Many different companies make printable fabric sheets, which are available in most craft or fabric stores as well as online. You can also make your own by ironing fabric to freezer paper (see page 27).

### Sewing Thread

Because of the combination of surfaces that I work with, I use machine quilting thread exclusively in my sewing machine. I'm fond of Coats & Clark for its strength as well as its economy.

### Tulle

Tulle's texture and color make it a mainstay in my fabric stash, and it does some amazing things under a heat gun!

## CRAFTING SUPPLIES AND TOOLS

### Flush Cutters

Flush cutters provide a nice straight cut on wire.

### Heat Gun

Any craft heat gun will work for your projects.

### Metal Rolls

For this book's projects I used 36-gauge copper, which can be trimmed down with metal shears or even scissors. (Do *not* use your fabric scissors!). The higher the gauge, the thinner the metal.

### Pens and Pencils

For projects where I am not concerned about washability, my favorite pen is LePen™ by Marvy®. It comes in a rainbow of colors and has a fine nib perfect for writing on fabric.

Graphite pencils are fantastic for writing on various surfaces, providing great definition without detracting from your work.

### Pliers

Chain nose pliers work well when you need to grip something or make a sharp bend in wire. Round nose pliers are used for making small loops and spirals as well as for wire wrapping.

### Punches

The revolving leather punch can penetrate just about anything, including many layers.

The Japanese screw punch is on the pricy side but worth the cost if you need to make holes through many layers for bookbinding.

### Rubber Stamps

Gather deeply etched stamps in all shapes and sizes.

### Transparency Film

There are many different brands of inkjet transparency film to choose from, and they can be purchased in most office supply stores. Make sure that you buy the kind of film that is specifically for ink-jet printers.

You can also purchase ready-to-use artistic transparencies online.

### Wire

Like metal, wire comes in various gauges. You can purchase brass, copper and steel wire in most hardware stores. The higher the gauge, the smaller the diameter of the wire. When beading, use a 24- or 26-gauge wire. For sturdier projects, use 18-gauge wire.

## PAINTS, DYES AND INKS

When I first started to alter fabrics, it was an extension of my painting, so I used whatever I had on hand. Now I often use less expensive craft paint.

Jacquard textile paint and Lumiere metallic paint have become my two favorite ways to stain fabric. To get a hint of glimmer, I add some Lumiere metallic paint to my base paint.

The size of my color bath is determined by the quantity of fabric that I want to stain. However, for the most part, I use 1 cup (.24l) of water, 3 teaspoons (15ml) of paint and 1 teaspoon (5ml) of metallic paint.

Tea and instant coffee are also wonderful mediums for dyeing fabric, especially if you want a natural look.

Of course, there are commercial dyes readily available at your local craft or fabric store. (I use RIT Dye.) Follow the manufacturer's instructions when using these. Also keep in mind that various types of fabric will each yield a different color effect within the same dye bath.

When stamping, StazOn® ink gives a good clean impression on fabric and dries almost instantly without smearing. VersaCraft® ink pads (formerly Fabrico) are for fabrics; images are washable when heat set. StazOn® and VersaCraft® are both made by Tsukineko and are available online. I use both inks; however, if I'm not creating something that needs to be washed, I favor StazOn® ink.

# section one:
# Offerings from *the* Heart

Handmade gifts really show how much you care. They're a way of sharing yourself with loved ones near and far, as the time you take to create something from your heart means oh so much. When you create one-of-a-kind gifts, you can add tiny details so the recipients know that you truly took the time to show how much you care and think about them.

A special book can be customized to the person's needs and taste while patterns and colors can be tailored to the recipient's personality. Personal keepsakes also can be incorporated into the piece such as a special photo or a few special beloved tokens.

Gift giving can be taken even further through innovative gift wrap that often becomes part of the gift itself. Scarves (that later can be worn) make a great wrapper for any fashion aficionado, whereas a vintage tea towel wrapped around a gift and tied with a length of lace would make the heart of a romantic flutter!

# scraps card

How many times have you found yourself in need of a gift card or a thank you note at the last minute? What if you're going out to lunch with a good friend and want a small card just to let that special someone know that she means the world to you?

With a few basic supplies and your inspiration jar (see page 14), you can have a card ready within minutes. Blank prefolded cards are now available at most craft stores as well as some discount stores, making this process very easy. Create one card—or an entire library of greeting cards—to keep on hand.

## GATHER THIS TO BEGIN

Brush (foam)

Cardstock (prefolded)

Dauber or make-up sponge

Decorative paper: book text

Embroidery floss, pearl cotton or thread (for ties)

Fabric: assorted scraps of organza, felt, others from your stash; muslin

Gel medium

Gesso (white)

Ink: stamp ink pad (brown)

Palette knife

Quilting machine needle, size 14/90

Quilting machine thread

Scissors

Sewing machine

1 » Rip a piece of muslin to fit the front of a folded card. Apply gesso over most of the piece of muslin.

2 » Stitch a heart shape on a scrap of organza and book text paper. (The sample pictured here was left over from the *Tree Art Project* on page 92.) Cut out the heart shape.

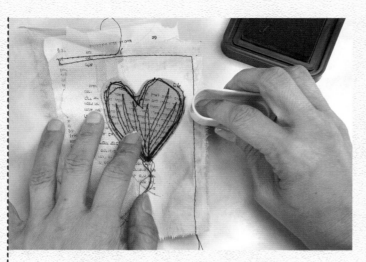

**3»** Layer the stitched heart with some other fabric scraps, book text and the gessoed muslin, and sew them all together. (I stitched along only 2 sides first, then sewed on the heart.) Use a dauber and some ink to "grunge up" the gessoed area of the main element a bit.

## INSPIRATION JAR

*At the end of a large project, when I begin the not-so-enjoyable task of cleaning up, the oddments on my table and floor often include treasures that generate many bright ideas. More often than not, these leftovers end up in a large glass jar that I keep close at hand. There they wait to find a new place within my artwork.*

*An inspiration jar is just the thing to move the creative process along. Simply reach into your holding place, pull out a few snippets and see how swiftly your ideas start to unfold.*

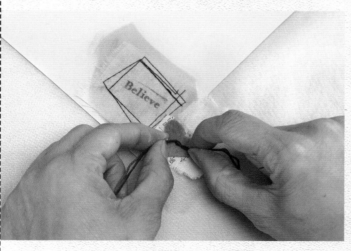

**4»** Create a little word patch to go inside of the card and stitch it to the bottom right corner. Tie on a felt heart.

## COLORS?
## THE CHOICE IS
## UP TO YOU

*As you glance over the materials lists for each project (Gather This To Begin), you'll see that often I don't suggest colors for felt, inks, embroidery floss or pearl cotton, etc. This is to allow you the freedom to make each project according to your own vision. Use the photos for each project as a guide in your color selections, or develop your own color palette. Explore your creativity!*

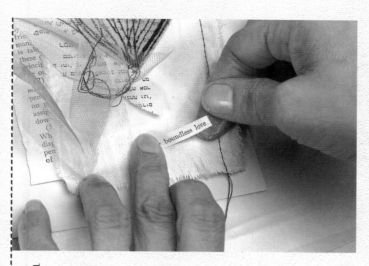

**5»** Use gel medium to add clipped text to the layered element for the front of the card. (Use text from the clip art on pages 122 and 123 or select other text that appeals to you.)

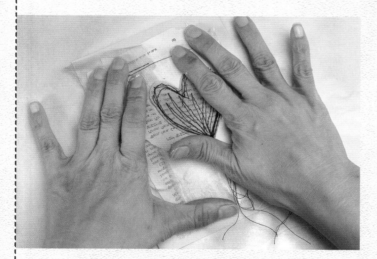

**6»** Glue the element to the front of the card using gel medium.

## ADDITIONAL TIPS

~ *Don't disregard any scraps you might have lying about. Almost anything can be incorporated into a card, even loose threads.*

~ *The juxtaposition of fabric and paper is always appealing. By simply adhering fabric to a postcard blank (or even a recycled card) and adding a few embellishments, you can create a card.*

~ *You can write on a card created from fabric quite easily with a suitable pen. When washability isn't a concern, I reach for LePen™ by Marvy®. Its fine nib is great for writing on fabric.*

# wired resin-paper card

Most of my fabric handiworks reflect my wire-working skills in some way, so naturally I devised wire frames for this project. They can be adapted to just about any size or shape with a few simple bends of the wire. While you're constructing your pieces, keep in mind that the wire eyes that attach each section together also help anchor each layer of the collage.

When you create a large batch of resin paper, spread it on an outdoor table to dry and cure overnight; just be sure to move it inside at night. (Lay it out near an open window for ventilation.) Keep a supply of this paper on hand; you will use it again and again as you discover innovative ways of integrating it into your art.

To create transparencies of your own images, buy ink-jet transparency film, available at most office supply stores. There's also an abundance of ready-made transparencies available for purchase online and in some art stores.

So, what are you waiting for? Go through your fabric, text and images, and play a bit with resin and transparencies. I promise you—once you begin this journey, you will be hooked!

## GATHER THIS TO BEGIN

Brush (foam)

Decorative paper: book text (several pages)

Fabric: scraps (dyed fabric, felt)

Embroidery floss

Flush cutter

Leather punch

Metal tray, cookie sheet or other heat-resistant surface

Needle (embroidery)

Pliers (chain nose, round nose)

Poster paint pen (Sharpie®)

Resin (2-part; I use Envirotex Lite®)

Transparency image

Trash bag (or other plastic to cover work surface)

Votive candle

Wire (16-gauge)

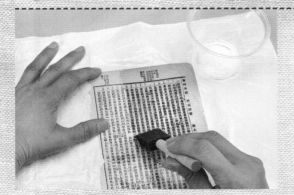

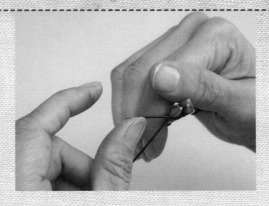

**1»** Mix 2-part resin following manufacturer's instruction. With a piece of plastic trash bag beneath for protection, apply resin over both sides of a piece of book text with a foam brush. Set the piece aside to cure overnight. Repeat for each resin text piece you need.

**2»** To make a 2½" x 3½" (6cm x 9cm) frame, start by cutting two 5" (13cm) and two 7" (18cm) lengths of steel wire. Leaving about a 2½" (6cm) tail on each of the 5" (13cm) pieces, create an eye loop on 1 end of each with round nose pliers.

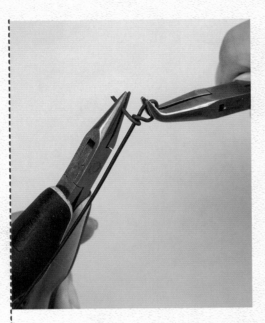

**3»** Holding each loop with chain nose pliers, use round nose pliers to wrap the tail wire around the base of the loop.

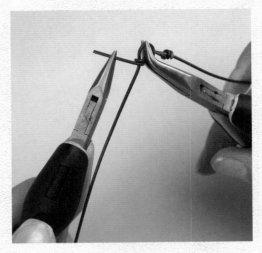

**4»** Create a loop on the end of one 7" (18cm) piece of wire. Thread the tail through the loop on a 5" (13cm) wire, then wrap the tail around the base of the loop you just created.

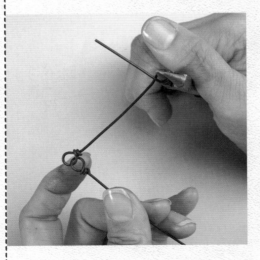

**5»** About 2" (5cm) from the other end of the first 5" (13cm) piece, form another loop with the round nose pliers. Wrap that tail wire around the loop.

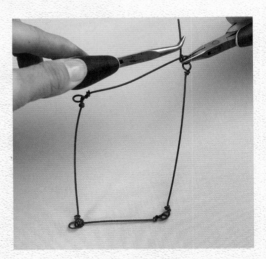

**6»** Make a loop at 1 end of the second piece of 7" (18cm) wire. Thread the tail through the second loop on the first 5" (13cm) wire piece, then wrap the tail around the base of the loop you just made. Continue in the same manner for the other 2 corners, connecting the loops in each corner to complete the 4-sided frame.

**7»** Print out your desired image onto ink-jet-compatible transparency material and trim it to size. Punch 1 or more holes into the transparency as a design element.

**8»** Light the candle and carefully begin melting the edges of the transparency. You need to set the plastic in the flame for only a second to ignite it, then shake it or blow it out before it burns too much. Repeat around the perimeter of the transparency. (See page 21 for advice about burning elements.)

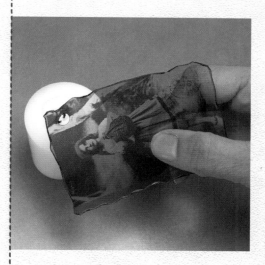

**9»** Hold the punched hole(s) over the flame, too. Burn or melt any additional areas as desired.

**10»** Peel the sheets of cured resin paper off of the trash bag. Create layers with the resin paper and various pieces of dyed fabric.

## TRY A VARIATION

*This project is easy to turn into a book. Simply tie fabric strips or ribbon to the top and bottom wire eye loops of the frame to create an accordian book (much like the Concertina Book on page 3o).*

**11»** On another piece of plain book text, find a word that you like. Cut a small slit in the resin paper where it would reveal the word on the book text when the resin paper is layered over it. Burn the resin layer carefully at the slit. (Remember to quickly blow out the flame.)

**12»** Burn the edges of the resin piece in the same manner as the transparency. Stack your layers: Tack the transparency onto your first piece of fabric, sewing it by hand with a needle and a thread in a contrasting color. Make the stitches themselves design elements. (Alternatively, you could sew these pieces together with a sewing machine.)

**13»** Layer the remaining pieces to complete the sandwich. The back of the card should show the resin paper with the burned window revealing the word you chose on the book text.

Next, layer in a piece of solid resin paper with the fabric/transparency layer on top. Cut a couple of small squares of felt and sandwich them over 1 corner. Sew through all layers at the corner to secure the entire sandwich.

## SEWING THROUGH LAYERS

*To make it easier to penetrate many layers of varied materials, I use the tabletop to help push the needle through.*

**14»** Stitch along 1 side of the card. When you get to a corner, attach the wire frame by securing the eye to the stacked layers. Add additional felt pieces at the remaining corners as well for extra security.

**15»** For a final layer of embellishment, doodle with a paint pen over the front of the transparency.

## ABOUT BURNING

*I primarily use two methods when burning art elements. The first is a tea light candle (plain, not dyed), the perfect size for singed edgings. The duration of flame to fabric is literally seconds (maybe 30 at most).*

*My second method is a heat gun, a contained method that allows control over burning speed once you find a comfortable "distance." The heat gun method is more about burning than finishing, so you can apply the heat for a longer duration (one to three minutes).*

*I sometimes use a butane lighter, also known as a barbeque lighter, when I want to burn a surface only, such as singeing away threads. This creates a wonderful aged appearance (see Ancestory Album, page 39).*

*Here are some additional tips for creative (and safe) burning:*

~ *Don't wear loose clothing, and pull your hair away from your face as an added safety measure.*

~ *If possible, burn outdoors for proper ventilation. Wear a mask, especially when burning synthetics as these emit hazardous fumes.*

~ *When burning, I place items on a cookie sheet for safety and to protect my work area.*

~ *Keep a small bowl of water close at hand when using an open flame.*

~ *In general, manmade fabrics melt very well; natural fabrics tend to smolder. A mix of synthetic and natural fibers along with paper or items with different heat tolerance will give you more control over your outcome.*

~ *When a fabric edge begins to smolder, extinguish it with the bowl of a metal spoon.*

~ *I often use a leather punch to create holes, then I singe the edges of the holes. A seam ripper is also helpful for creating depth and opening up areas to be burned.*

~ *Always stop at various points to look over your work before continuing the burning process.*

# art GIRL DOLL and apron

Imagine the countless *Art Girls* you can bring together with this simple doll pattern (see page 116). The ideas are limited only by your imagination!

When I had the idea to make this doll, I wanted to share how you could use an image of yourself or a loved one for the face. Sadly, the prototypes fell short of my intended vision. However, if the idea of putting a familiar face on your doll appeals to you, by all means play away. All you need to do is print a facial image (from a photo of you or a loved one) onto purchased printer fabric sheets. You can also create your own printable fabric by ironing freezer paper to fabric, then cutting it to the size that will fit your printer (see page 27). After you have printed the face you wish to use, cut it out and sew it to the doll's head prior to stitching the body together.

By placing wire directly into the doll's body and small magnets in the tips of her hands and feet, you will be able to pose your doll in whatever manner you wish. With hand-dyed muslin in a wide range of shades, you can make *Art Girls* in just about every color. Girls young and old will surely delight in your creations!

*Art Girl* doll garments are not just clothing items—they're works of art unto themselves! Art doll clothing can be made in just about any size; with the use of fabric dyes and inks, you can turn it into a life-size wearable piece of art. Details are important when you create these diminutive pieces. Combine vintage lace and fabrics for a timeworn effect. See *Making Doll Clothes* on page 26 for more information; pages 117–119 include patterns for the apron, a dress and a special wings element.

## GATHER THIS TO BEGIN

Buttons (2)

Decorative paper: sheet music or book text

Dowel or round marking pen (for shaping wire)

Embroidery floss (variegated red)

Fabric: muslin (1 yard [1m]); organza

Fiberfill

Flush cutter

Freezer paper or prefabricated fabric sheets for printer

Ink: VersaCraft® or fabric ink (black)

Mini clothespins

Needle (hand-sewing)

Patterns (Doll, page 116; Apron, page 117)

Pencil

Pins

Quilting machine needle, size 14/90

Quilting machine thread

Rubber stamps (deeply etched facial and script designs, or any designs of choice)

Scissors

Seam binding or ribbon

Sewing machine

Thread (regular)

Trim: rickrack, lace or other

Wire (16-gauge and 18-gauge)

## MAKE THE DOLL

**1»** Iron a 1-yard (91cm) piece of muslin, then trace the doll pattern onto it. Stamp over the muslin with text stamps, filling in all areas of the pattern. I like to use a face stamp for the doll's face. (To use a photo instead, see the project introduction on page 23.)

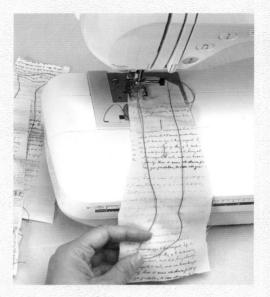

**2»** Pin the stamped muslin to another piece of muslin the same size. Leaving a margin around each outline, loosely cut out the doll's body parts. Sew around the pattern lines for each individual piece except for the flat ends of the arms and legs and the bottom line of the body—leave those unsewn.

**3»** Stamp the backs of all of the sewn pieces. Trim the pieces to ⅛" (3mm) beyond the sewn line.

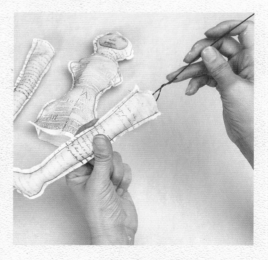

**4»** Add fiberfill stuffing to each of the pieces. If you like, you can insert a length of 18-gauge wire into each piece to make the doll poseable.

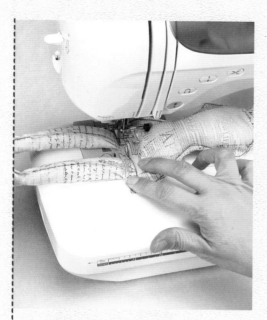

**5»** Insert the ends of the legs into the bottom of the doll's body and sew the body closed. (Make certain the wire is not in the way when you're sewing.)

**6»** Sew up the arms independent of the doll's body.

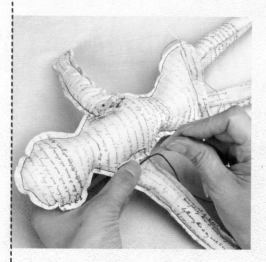

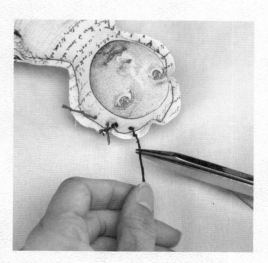

**7»** Hand-stitch the arms to the back of the body. I like to add a button at each arm joint.

**8»** For hair, thread a knotted piece of floss through a small portion of the head. Tie another knot; use a pin or needle to move the knot close to the head, then cut the floss. Repeat for as many strands of hair as you would like.

## MAKE THE APRON

**1»** Copy and cut out the pattern on page 117 and trace it onto a piece of sheet music, book text or other decorative paper.

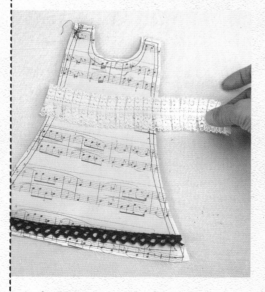

**3»** Cut out the apron 1/8" beyond the sewing line. Try out different pieces of trim to see what looks good.

**2»** Sandwich the marked paper between 2 layers of organza and sew around the traced line.

## MAKING DOLL CLOTHES

*You can fashion patterns using either your own body shape or your doll's (or use the patterns provided on pages 117-119). Pencil sketch your design directly onto the fabric or tracing paper. Often I find inspiration in children's clothing as it has the simplest lines to follow. Fabric can be sewn with wrong sides together, leaving a raw edge exposed, which will create a chic grunge look.*

*If you choose, sew the garments with the right sides together, which will create an inside seam. If you do this, be sure to leave proper room for a seam allowance when developing your pattern. Once the piece is sewn, turn it right side out.*

*Also keep in mind that any surface treatment is best added before you stitch your clothing; this allows you to sew and embellish your fabric with greater ease.*

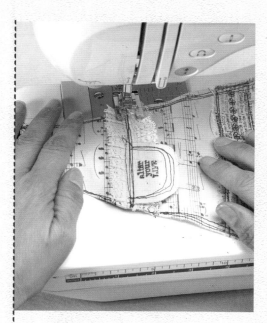

**4»** Sew on your chosen trim plus extras like the pocket for the apron. (Copy and cut out the pattern on page 117.)

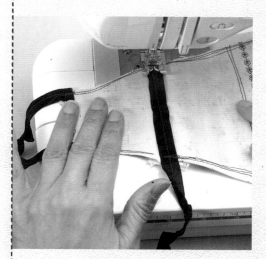

**6»** Sew the ribbon to the apron as ties at the waist and top.

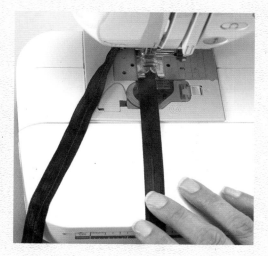

**5»** Embellish a piece of ribbon simply by sewing down the center of it.

## FREEZER PAPER FUSION METHOD

*You can use just about any kind of fabric that can be heated with an iron to create printable fabric. Cut a piece of fabric sized to fit through your printer. Place the fabric right side down on the ironing surface. Center the freezer paper, shiny side down, over the fabric and iron until the freezer paper is bonded to the fabric. (Use a dry iron with a cotton setting.) Turn the sheet over and iron on the fabric side, removing any wrinkles. Let the bonded fabric sit at least five minutes prior to running it through your printer. As with all electronic equipment, be sure to refer to your printer's instruction manual prior to doing this.*

## MAKE THE HANGER

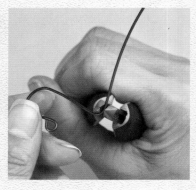

**1»** To make a hanger for your doll clothes, start with a 14" (36cm) length of 16-gauge wire. Make a loop on 1 end using round nose pliers.

**2»** Curve the wire around a dowel or a pen.

**3»** Using chain nose pliers, create a 90° bend in the wire.

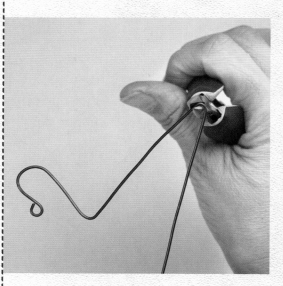

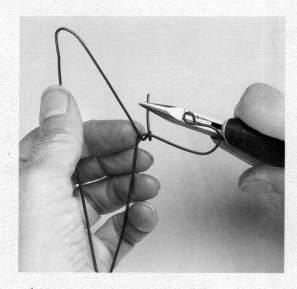

**4»** Make a second bend about 2½" (6cm) from the first bend.

**5»** Bend the wire again about 4" (10cm) beyond the second bend. Finally, wrap the excess wire around the neck of the hanger.

**7»** You can now hang your item of clothing on its own hanger.

**6»** To make them more interesting, stamp onto the miniature clothespins you'll use to attach the garment to the hanger.

## GIFT CARD

*Create a gift card easily with a piece of heavy card stock folded in half. Sew the wire hanger that holds the dress to the front of the card with a strand of embroidery floss.*

# concertina BOOK

This delightfully straightforward book can become just about anything you want it to be. The *Concertina Book* has a simplistic form that can be altered effortlessly in a multitude of ways suited to just about any need or theme.

Family photos can be printed onto specially treated fabric for ink-jet printers (available in most craft and fabric stores or online). Or you can make your own with freezer paper and regular fabric (see page 27). Photos of flowers from your garden or of a family pet would be equally delightful. Just think of the joy you could bestow on new parents or grandparents with photos of their little ones compiled into a book made just for them! You could even try to incorporate a few pieces of the children's outgrown clothing in the pages, building in an additional layer of sentiment.

The ideas are never-ending as are the embellishments that you can use—the foldout format allows you to add on the layers with ease. Because of the nature of the folds in the book, there is no need to worry about the thickness of your pages. Just let your imagination run wild and create your own masterpiece.

## GATHER THIS TO BEGIN

Acrylic paint (golden iridescent bronze)

Brush (foam)

Embellishments (assorted)

Eyelets (sixteen ¼" [6mm]) and setter

Fabric: felt (craft or wool) in complementary colors; muslin; other scraps as desired

Fabric glue stick

Fiberfill

Four 4" × 6" [10cm × 15cm] pieces heavy cardstock, thin cardboard or Grungeboard (Tim Holtz idea-ology)

Freezer paper or prefabricated fabric sheets for printer

Images of your choice

Ink: VersaCraft® or fabric ink (dark brown)

Iron and ironing board (optional)

Paper towels

Quilting machine needle, size 14/90

Quilting machine thread

Rubber stamp (text)

Sewing machine

Trim: lace

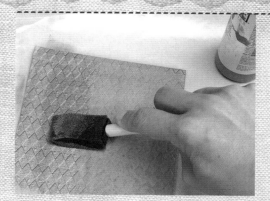

**1»** Apply gold acrylic paint with a foam brush to both sides of all 4 pieces of board. Work in small sections at a time.

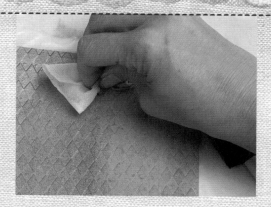

**2»** With a paper towel, quickly rub the paint off before it dries or seeps into the board too much. Do this for all 4 boards.

**3»** Stamp onto the dried boards with a text stamp.

**4»** Set two ¼" (6mm) eyelets into the corners on the right side of the front cover board and 2 into the corners on the left side of the back cover board. Set the same eyelets into each of the 4 corners on each remaining board. Make sure that the position of the holes correspond on all of the boards.

**5»** Create 8 collages, 1 for each side of each board. Assemble your first collage, laying out assorted scraps of lace, felt, fabric and embellishments. If you would like to use the same images I have used here, scan them from pages 122 and 123 and print them onto muslin using the freezer paper fusion method (see page 27).

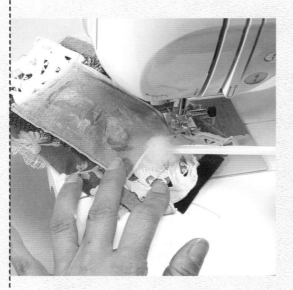 

**6»** Once your collage is layered as you would like it, machine-sew it together. Start with the layers beneath the main image. Next, sew 3 sides of the main image, then stuff the image a little with fiberfill.

**7»** Sew the fourth side of the main image. To add a bit of texture, I like to sew around all 4 sides a couple more times.

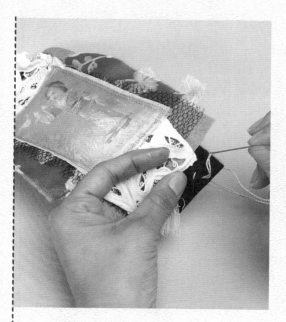

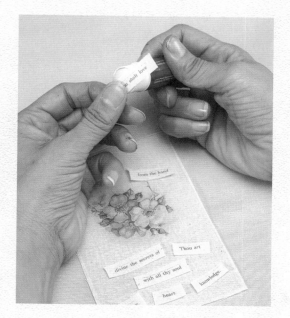

**8»** Hand-sew final touches, such as adding decorative stitches or buttons.

**9»** Create the collage that goes on the backside of the page. If you are using a collage with small pieces of text, first adhere them to the collage with a fabric glue stick before stitching them into place.

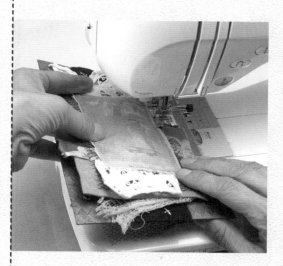

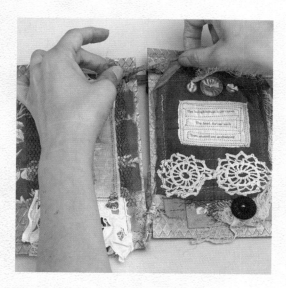

**10»** Again, start with the bottom layers, machine-stitching them down. Next, secure all of the words on the image piece. Finally, sew the image piece to the layers piece, adding a bit of fiberfill if you like.

Sew 1 collage onto 1 piece of Grunge-board. Turn the piece over and sew the other collage on the backside. Be careful to avoid sewing through the eyelets.

**11»** Repeat for the remaining pieces of board, creating a collage for each side. Tie the pages together using strips torn from scraps of the fabric you used in the collages. Stamp on some pieces or not—it's up to you.

# MELANGE JOURNAL

Looking for a place to write down your hopes and dreams? Need a bit of encouragement to start your own art journal? Consider this project a permission slip to start your personal journey into journaling. Or it can be a great gift for the journalist in your life. I have found when I create a journal I am more apt to work in it as the entire piece becomes a personal work of art.

Journaling is a process of creating all in itself. Our words, thoughts and memories become intertwined together when placed on the blank page, creating their own mosaic. A treasured journal that is by itself a piece of art is not only inspirational but loved when filled with glimpses from our lives.

I like to combine sewing and fabric into my journal, adding layers upon layers of textures that will then serve as further inspiration when I begin to journal. Often I will journal my page outside of the book and then, with book-binding glue and a palette knife, I will evenly coat the back and adhere it directly to the page. The use of a brayer is helpful in pressing your page into your journal as it will increase pressure.

## GATHER THIS TO BEGIN

Acrylic paint (I used Golden's green gold)

Binder clips

Bone folder

Bookbinder's awl

Buttons

Cardstock

Decorative papers

Fabric: assorted scraps; cheesecloth; felt (craft or wool); muslin; organza

Fiberfill

Fusible web (heavy duty)

Ink: StazOn®

Needle (tapestry)

Quilting machine needle, size 14/90

Quilting machine thread

Rubber stamps

Ruler

Scissors

Sewing machine

Trim: lace

20 pieces 11" × 17" (28cm × 43cm) 140 lb. watercolor paper

Waxed linen (yellow)

1» Cut two 11" × 19" (28cm × 48cm) felt pieces. Iron fusible web between them. Tear 2 pieces of decorative paper to fit the front and back covers, 1 to fit the spine. Position all 3 on the felt. Cut organza to layer over the entire piece, then straight stitch around to secure.

2» For the 2" (5cm) spine, measure 8½" (22cm) in from the edges of the front and back covers. Sew straight stitches from top to bottom on either side of the spine paper piece.

**3»** Dye several scraps of different types of fabric, lace and/or cheesecloth, using acrylic paint and water (see page 9). Create a decorative element for the front cover by layering dyed fabric scraps and an altered paper element (such as the rose card here that I further decorated with rubber stamps). Be sure to leave space to add buttons in Step 4. Machine-stitch the layers together.

**4»** Stitch the dyed-scrap piece to the front cover. Add buttons to empty spaces on the front cover or place them as you see fit.

On the inside cover, hand- or machine-stitch pockets cut from muslin you've printed with a rubber stamp (words or other design).

**5»** Make tabs by tearing muslin into 1" × 5" (3cm × 13cm) strips. Print over 1 strip with a background stamp. Fold the stamped muslin strip in half, then stamp with a word stamp of your choice. Leaving open about ½" (13mm) opposite the folded side of the tab, sew the tab together on 3 sides. Stuff the tab with a bit of fiberfill and sew the final side closed. Repeat for the remaining tabs.

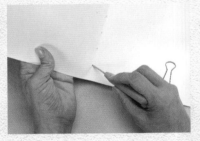

**6»** Cut twenty 11" × 17" (28cm × 43cm) pieces of cold-press watercolor paper (or cardstock); fold each piece in half using a bone folder. Position the first tab as desired along the edge of 1 of the folded watercolor pages.

**7»** Sew the outside edge of the page several times to secure the tab. (Do not sew the folded page shut.) Repeat for the remaining tabs.

**8»** Stack the sheets, opened flat, into 4 signatures of 5 sheets each, with tabbed sheets positioned where you want them.

Secure pages of 1 signature together with a binder clip. Starting 1" (3cm) from the top, mark 10 vertical dots 1" (3cm) apart down the length of the fold. With an awl, punch a hole through the stack of 5 sheets at each dot. Repeat for the remaining signatures.

**9»** Beginning 1" (3cm) from the top of the spine, mark dots in 4 vertical rows that are spaced ½" (13mm) apart. Each vertical row should contain 10 dots spaced 1" (3cm) apart down the spine.

With an awl, pierce a hole through each dot on the spine (40 holes).

**10»** To sew the signatures into the spine, begin by threading a tapestry needle with 36" (91m) of waxed linen knotted at 1 end. Insert the needle through the bottom hole in the fold of the first signature, then through the first hole at the bottom of the first vertical row on the inside right of the spine. Pull the thread taut to the knot.

**11»** Cross the spine to insert the needle through the second hole from the bottom of the second vertical row. Bring the needle through the second hole in the fold of the second signature.

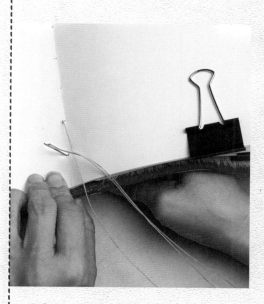

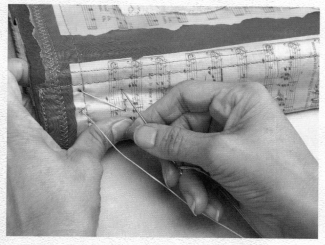

**12»** Bring the needle down through the first hole in the fold of the second signature.

**13»** Push the needle through the bottom hole of the second vertical row on the spine. Cross the spine to the first vertical row. Insert the needle in the second hole from the bottom, then guide the needle through the second hole in the first signature's fold.

Repeat this pattern up the length of the spine until the first 2 signatures are sewn. You should have 5 large Xs on the spine; the waxed linen makes its final pass through the top hole in the first signature's fold. Knot the waxed linen close to the hole and cut.

Repeat the whole process with the second set of 2 signatures, sewing through the third and fourth vertical rows in the spine. You should finish with 5 horizontal pairs of sewn Xs.

# ancestory ALBUM

I made this piece in 2005 as a gift for my mother. It holds photos of *her* mother shortly before she boarded a boat in 1912 to join her husband in America—a journey to a new life and a new legacy. (See *Famico's Legacy* on page 43.)

My sister discovered these photos; my grandmother had never shared them with us prior to her death at 98. I used them in this album to piece together a narrative of her life so her legacy would live on. Your album could include pockets for letters, photos and family jewelry, and you could work in cloth from family member's garments. (I made the brooch on the album cover from notions from my grandmother's sewing box.) Imagine the elements you could combine to make a family treasure!

## GATHER THIS TO BEGIN

Acrylic paint (gold)

Beads (assorted)

Bone folder

Brush (foam)

Butane lighter (optional)

Buttons (of choice)

Cardstock

Decorative paper: book text or sheet music

Eyelets (1/8") and setter

Fabric: decorative (such as brocade); felt (I used washed wool felt, see page 8); natural muslin; organza

Flush cutter

Freezer paper or prefabricated fabric sheets for printer

Images on fabric, or transparencies for ink-jet printers

Ink: StazOn® (Dark Brown)

Iron and ironing board (optional)

Japanese screw punch or bookbinder's awl

3 lobster clasps

Mementos (of choice, assorted)

Metal tray, cookie sheet or other heat-resistant surface

Needle (embroidery and tapestry)

Paper towels or baby wipes

Pearl cotton #5 (or embroidery floss)—color according to your palette (I used cream)

Pliers (chain nose, round nose)

Quilting machine needle, size 14/90

Quilting machine thread

Rubber stamps (deeply etched designs that work well with your theme)

Scissors

Sewing machine

Trim: lace or other as desired

Waxed linen

Wire (20-gauge and 24-gauge)

**1»** Cut a 6½" × 9½" (17cm × 24cm) piece of cardstock. Using a bone folder, score a vertical line 1½" (4cm) from 1 end of the cardstock. Fold the cardstock over and burnish it in both directions with the bone folder.

**2»** Pick a fabric for the cover and cut a 7" x 18" (18cm x 46cm) piece. Create a layered embellishment and sew it to the right half of the fabric.

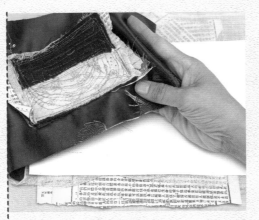

**3»** Lay the cover fabric face down. Over the bottom half, layer various papers and fabrics to peek out of the edges; also insert the scored cardstock, with the fold near the center of the cover fabric. Fold the top half of the cover fabric down over the layers.

Sew around the perimeter of the cover. At 1½" (4cm) from the fold in the cover fabric, stitch a line to correspond with the scored cardstock line beneath it. (This creates a "hinge" for the cover.)

Repeat Steps 1–3 to create a back cover; the layered embellishment will be inside the back cover.

**4»** Trim a piece of cardstock to 6" × 16" (15cm × 41cm) and fold in half. Apply gold paint over and around the fold, then wipe off the excess with a baby wipe or a paper towel.

**5»** When the paint is dry, fold the cardstock in half, then fold it again 1½" (4cm) from the center fold. Burnish with the bone folder.

Repeat, making 1 folded piece of cardstock for every 4 fabric pages you're planning for your book.

**6»** Begin creating the pages to represent your ancestors. Each page can display a different technique and treatment. Here, I start with a photo printed on a transparency. (I'm burning the edges using a butane lighter.)

**7»** Layer the photo over stamped fabric and sew it to a piece of 6" × 9" (15cm × 23cm) felt, leaving 1 side of the transparency open. Insert a memento or 2 (like the pearls I used here) into the open side. Sew the fourth side shut.

**8»** Add hand-stitched details like the French knots I'm making here.

**9»** Begin working on the page that will back the one you just finished. For this page try printing your photo on some silk (*Freezer Paper Fusion Method*, page 27). Sew the silk onto felt to create a stuffed tag. Leave an opening for stuffing.

For this tag, I wanted to tie on a ribbon with some interest, so I first stamped the ribbon.

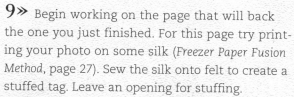

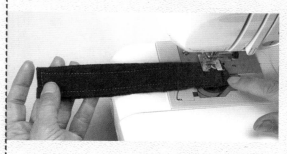

**10»** After you have stuffed the tag and sewn it shut, tie on the stamped ribbon.

**11»** Sew the tag to a new 6" × 9" (15cm × 23cm) piece of felt. Again, finish the page with some decorative embroidery or add embellishments. Sometimes I add blanket stitches to the edges, too. It's all up to you.

Create the next 2 pages in the same manner, using more photos and whatever materials or techniques that you wish. When 4 pages are complete, sew them to the painted cardstock to create a signature: Match the first 2 felt-backed pages, wrong sides together, with ½ of the cardstock sheet between them, and sew all 3 layers together. Repeat for the other 2 pages and the other half of the cardstock sheet.

**12»** Fold the completed signature back in half along the fold line on the cardstock. Complete however many more pages you wish, then cut the same number of 2" × 7" (5cm × 18cm) strips of felt. Fold each strip in half, then sew to secure.

**13»** Starting 2" (5cm) from 1 end of a sewn felt strip, mark 4 holes every 1" (3cm), leaving 2" (5cm) at the other end.

Stack the book pages, starting with the bottom cover with the layered element facing upward. Add a felt strip as a spacer, then a folded signature, another spacer and so on, with the marked spacer on top. With a Japanese hole punch, make holes at the spacer marks working with several layers at a time. Also use the marked spacer to punch holes in the front cover, then stack the front cover over the spacer. Make sure the layered element is facing up.

**14»** Thread a tapestry needle with about 40" (102cm) of waxed linen. Insert the needle from the bottom through the first hole (far left) in the top spacer. Pull it through and tie the linen at the outside edge of the album.

**15»** Bring the needle back through the first hole from the back. Align a stick along the spine of the album. Bring the thread over the stick, down around the stack and up through the second hole.

Bring the thread around the stack again and come up through the third hole; repeat with the fourth hole.

At the bottom of the spine, bring the thread around the outside of the book (as you did when starting the first knot) and come up through the fourth hole from the back again.

**16»** Stitch back down the spine, bringing the thread around the stick and the stack again, crossing over the first series of stitches, and ending at the first hole.

### CREATING THE BEADED TASSEL

*Start with a small strand of knotted linen; add beads and a charm on one end. Cut several lengths of fibers and stamped fabrics to about 3" (8cm). Cut 12" (30cm) of 24-gauge wire and make a wrapped eye at one end. Hold the eye at the center of the bundle of strips and linen and wrap the wire around the bundle several times.*

**17»** Tie off the thread using the original tail. Make sure all of your stitches are taut.

**18»** If you made a lot of pages for your book, chances are your book is chunky. To create a closure, start by setting an eyelet centered near the edge of both the back and the front cover. On the front cover, thread a 5" (13cm) length of 20-gauge wire through the eyelet.

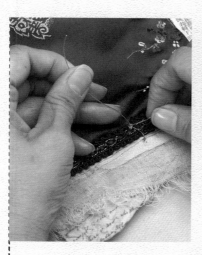

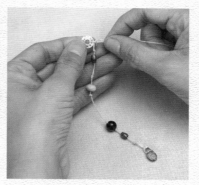

**19»** Twist the wire together.

**20»** Trim the excess wire from the shorter of the 2 pieces, then use chain nose pliers to create an eye and wrap the tail around the base of the loop.

**21»** Trim the excess, then repeat for the back cover, adding a lobster clasp before closing the loop.

Make a bracelet of rosary-wrapped beads that includes a decorative tassel. (See page 103 for directions on how to rosary-wrap a bead; see the sidebar on page 42 for directions on how to make a beaded tassel.)

**22»** Thread on about 8 small pearls or seed beads. After the wire has been folded to create a cap for the tassel, wrap the wire around the top of the bundle.

## FAMICO'S LEGACY

*My great-grandmother Famico, whom we called o-baa-chan, came from Japan to the United States to wed when she was just 15. During World War II, Famico and Aisso, along with their three children, were imprisoned at Manzanar. They were allowed to take only what they could carry with them. Three years later, in 1945, they were released, but the price my great-grandmother paid was the loss of her husband, who had died in camp from complications of appendicitis. Famico's family in Japan begged her to return, but she chose to stay in California to raise her family.*

*Famico kept much of her true self hidden from us. Looking back is never a choice in a Japanese household; we learn from an early age to look only toward tomorrow. This is a positive way to lead one's life, but it would have been nice if Famico had shared more of her personal legacy. One's family history is best written by those who lived it.*

**23»** Trim the excess wire and attach the tassel to 1 end of the bracelet. Use the lobster clasps to secure the bracelet to the book and to keep the book closed.

# masking paper gift mailer

During the process of creating a gift, I find my mind wandering to the gift wrapping portion of the presentation. I begin to ponder just how I will be sending my precious cargo out into the world.

Since I am eternally on the lookout for items that can be repurposed into my art, I have a rather large stockpile of such things as wax paper and sheet music. I find the combination of these two items creates a fast and easy gift wrap that's beautiful and leaves a lasting impression.

I discovered painter's masking paper when we remodeled our home. An abundance of leftover rolls made me contemplate how I could work this paper into my art. I absolutely adored the soft mossy green color as well as the texture (not to mention the durable nature of it).

Take a look around your studio. You, too, might find all kinds of discards and unexpected materials that can become lovely gift wrap.

## GATHER THIS TO BEGIN

Decorative paper: sheet music or other

Gift to be mailed

Glue stick

Masking paper*

Quilting machine needle, size 14/90

Quilting machine thread

Scissors

Sewing machine

Wax paper

*I use masking papers from 3M. They offer 6 different roll sizes in white, brick, green (my favorite) and gold.*

1 » Sandwich a piece of sheet music or other decorative paper between 2 sheets of wax paper. Sew around the perimeter.

2 » Fold the paper over and sew up the sides.

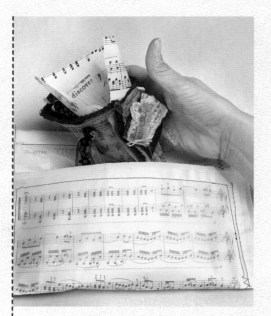

**3»** Insert your gift.

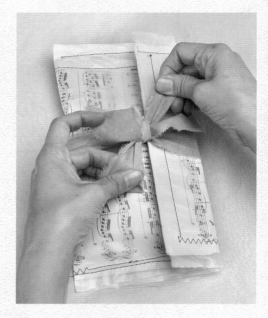

**4»** Tie on a pretty bow.

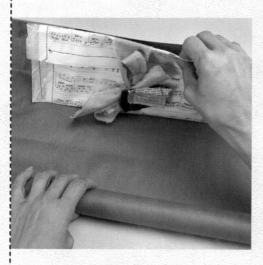

**5»** Add any additional embellishments to the wrapping, then roll the gift a few times in masking paper.

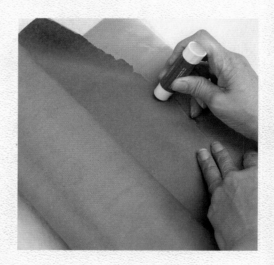

**6»** Glue the edge of the masking paper closed with a glue stick.

## PROTECTING
## YOUR GIFT

*If you're shipping during the winter months, wrap your gift in a layer of plastic food wrap or place it in a zipper storage bag to help protect it from the elements.*

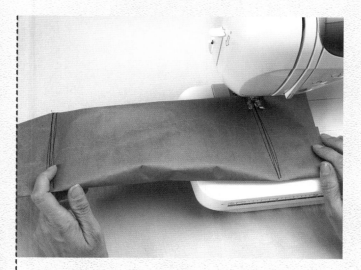

**7»** Position the gift inside the paper at 1 end, then sew up the opposite end of the mailer. Push the gift toward the sewn end to give it a little wiggle room, then sew up the other side of the mailer.

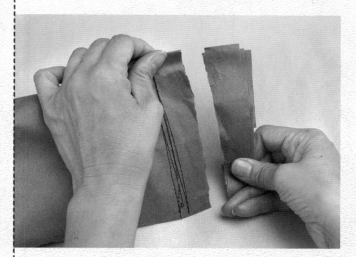

**8»** Tear off the excess paper.

## MASKING PAPER AS GIFT WRAP

*I first used masking paper as it was intended, taping it down to protect my tabletop as I painted or stamped. One day I needed to wrap something for shipping. I was out of brown craft paper, so I reached for a masking paper roll. Soon I discovered that it was perfect for wrapping an odd-sized gift. The color was luscious, and the paper was flexible yet sturdy enough to run through the sewing machine. Masking paper provides a supplement to your normal assortment of gift wrap—durable and flexible, yet attractive and alterable.*

# STITCHED-FROM-THE-HEART GIFT WRAP

Japanese gift wrapping, called *tsutsumi* ("wrapping") or *furoshiki* ("wrapping with cloth"), was commonplace in my family. The Japanese equate wrapping a gift with "wrapping the heart"—visual and beautiful on the outside, married to the expression of simplicity, balance and nature.

I often combine two materials when creating gift wrap, as texture adds depth and interest. Incorporating papers and fabrics creates an amazing juxtaposition. Often scraps from the main project find their way into my gift wrapping, adding another layer that relates to the gift itself.

Everyday items become narrative when incorporated into gift wrapping. Use contrasting colors and textures, combine rustic elements, like sticks and seed pods, with the eternal—the earthy alongside the sublime is a combination that speaks volumes.

## GATHER THIS TO BEGIN

Fabric: felt; tulle or organza

Needle (embroidery)

Pearl cotton #5
(or embroidery floss)

Scissors

**1»** Start with a felt rectangle large enough to wrap around your gift item from both directions. Place your item in the center at a 45° angle.

Fold up 1 side, then an adjacent side with the end turned under. Start stitching the package together.

**2»** Tie off the thread and proceed to the next side; fold that in and secure with additional stitches. Proceed to the fourth side, folding and stitching until the gift item is completely wrapped.

**3»** Tie the package with frayed lengths of organza and/or tulle. Add a handmade gift tag, if you like.

# vintage-modern gift cone

Gift cones can be made in any size. They can be simple or completely dressed up in an over-the-top fashion. Vintage lace, trim and rhinestone jewelry, as well as cording and tassels, heighten the drama to create enticing masterpieces.

With the use of fabric dye, inks and paints, this project goes from average to extraordinary, transforming a Victorian cone from traditional to vintage-modern with a twist. Simple adornments as well as trinkets and treasures tucked within create a vignette of beauty and grace.

I made these small "words of wisdom" gift cones as a way to reach out to a special someone with a little "just because" gift. Small tokens such as a short note or a nugget of wisdom can be slipped into these cones. Even a fortune from a cookie or a ticket stub from a shared event can be included for increased sentiment.

## GATHER THIS TO BEGIN

2–5 beads (assorted)

Decorative paper: book text or sheet music

Emery board

Fabric: assorted scraps; cheesecloth; dyed muslin; dyed shop towels

Feather (any color)

Flat marble

Gel medium

Ink: StazOn® or fabric ink (black)

Leather punch

Needle (embroidery)

Quilting machine needle, size 14/90

Quilting machine thread

Pearl cotton #5 (or embroidery floss) in any color that works with your palette

Rubber stamps (deeply etched designs of choice)

Scissors

Sewing machine

Trim: lace and other assorted

**1»** Cut a scrap of muslin, dyed to your preferred color, into a rectangle or square and stamp onto it.

**2»** Cut a dyed shop towel just slightly larger than the muslin. Sew the 2 pieces together by running a stitch around the perimeter a few times.

**3»** Create a small element (such as this heart that I cut from the dyed shop towel and a bit of cheesecloth). Position it at a 45° degree angle in the center of the stamped side of the piece and sew it into place.

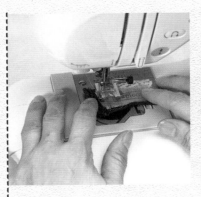  

**4 »** Create a little word tag using a few layers of fabric scraps or lace and a stamped word.

**5 »** Bring 2 adjacent sides of the rectangle together and sew it closed.

**6 »** By hand, tack the seam over to the side a bit and sew on the little word tag.

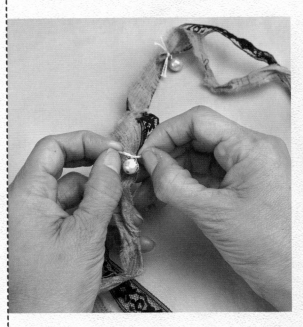 

**7 »** Cut two pieces of trim about 18" (46cm) long. Tie a few stamped, wire-wrapped pearls around the strands to hold them together.

**8 »** Punch 2 holes at opposite sides of the cone's top about 1" (3cm) down from the edge.

## ABOUT GIFT CONES

*Gift cones have been a mainstay in society since Queen Victoria. They have been used to decorate as well as to present gifts during holidays and celebrations, filled with everything from flowers and candy to trinkets and baubles.*

**9»** Thread the combined trim strand through the holes from the inside to the outside, then tie a knot at each end of the strand to secure it as a hanger/handle.

**10»** Create an enclosure by stamping onto the top of a feather.

**11»** For another enclosure, find a word that appeals to you on a piece of book text. Adhere a clear flat marble over the word with gel medium.

**12»** When the medium is dry, cut around the marble and sand off the excess paper with an emery board.

## A CONE FOR ALL SEASONS

*The cone shape adapts well to every season—a Christmas tree cone can be re-created easily for spring. Although perfect for holding a gift, the cone itself can become the gift. Gift cones look pretty hanging on a wall, a door handle or even a wreath. Dry flowers or lavender make a lovely addition.*

**13»** To provide more stability for the finished cone, cut a piece of decorative paper the same size as the original muslin piece and form it into a cone shape. Slide it into the fabric cone, then add your enclosures.

# SECTION TWO:
# Reflections of *the* Soul

Developing and executing a piece of art is a truly personal experience. Wearing and using that art in daily life is an extension of one's soul.

The projects in this section are incredibly personal, each one allotting as much meaning as the creator wishes to include. There are treasured moments that we all wish to carry with us: A shell we found on the beach takes us back to the childhood days of our grown children, while a decorative banner reminds us of that which motivates and drives us. A piece of jewelry adorned with endearing sentiments warms our hearts when we wear it, while a favorite apron reminds us to let the beauty we love be seen in what we do.

Any one of these projects is your chance to share a glance into your soul with those around you.

# art-on-your-wrist cuff bracelet

Why not wear your art on your wrist? Wrist cuffs are a wonderful way to use cast-off strips of fabric, ribbon and even paper from previous projects. It's also a way to highlight a special button or give a piece of old jewelry new life.

Imagine a cuff constructed completely of delicate vintage lace sewn onto leather—the juxtaposition of textures would be amazing. Or use a computer to work with words and images, then print your design onto printable fabric, either store-bought or homemade. (See page 27 for *Freezer Paper Fusion Method* instructions.)

To help protect your art cuff from wear and tear, spray on a fabric protector following manufacturer's instructions. Be sure to allow ample drying time prior to wearing your new creation.

Once you make one of these unique bracelets, many more are sure to follow.

## GATHER THIS TO BEGIN

Beading needle and thread

Beads (pearls)

Buttons

Computer with scanner

Fabric: cheesecloth (dyed); felt (craft or wool, any color); muslin

Freezer paper or prefabricated fabric sheets for printer

Ink: StazOn®, VersaCraft® or fabric ink (black)

Iron and ironing board

Needle (embroidery)

Pearl cotton #5 (or embroidery floss)

Printer

Quilting machine needle, size 14/90

Quilting machine thread

Rubber stamps (script or decorative)

Scissors

Seam ripper

Sewing machine

**1»** Using StazOn® or VersaCraft® black ink (or fabric ink), stamp a script stamp or other decorative design onto a piece of muslin.

**2»** Cut two 1½" × 8½" (4cm x 22cm) pieces of felt. Cut a piece of dyed cheese-cloth about the same size. Scrunch up the cheesecloth a bit and secure it to 1 of the felt pieces with a series of free-form, back-and-forth machine stitches.

**3»** Tear the stamped muslin into 3 small scraps. Stitch around the perimeter of each scrap to secure it to the cuff.

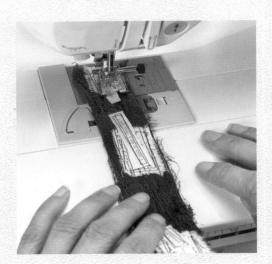

**4»** Fuse a piece of muslin to a piece of freezer paper. Choose words to scan from the clip art on pages 122 and 123 and print them onto printable fabric or fused muslin (see page 27). Cut out 3 words and sew them randomly to the cuff.

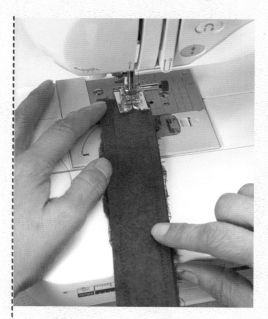

**5»** To finish the cuff nicely and conceal the stitches that show on the reverse, sew the second piece of felt to the wrong side of the first, stitching around the perimeter.

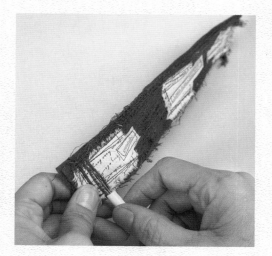

**6»** Using your machine's buttonhole attachment, add a buttonhole to 1 end of the cuff, sizing the hole to fit your chosen button. Cut the hole open with a seam ripper, starting at the center and ripping in 1 direction, then the other.

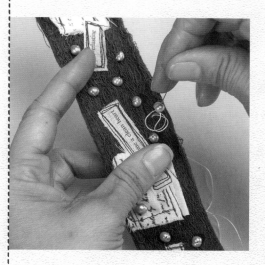

**7»** Use a beading needle and beading thread to sew on the pearls. Do not sew through the bottom layer of felt.

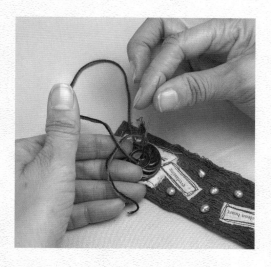

**8»** For the final step, sew a button on the opposite end of the cuff from the buttonhole using thread, embroidery floss or pearl cotton. (I like to tie the thread so it shows on the top of the button.)

# BUTTONHOLE ALTERNATIVES

*If you choose to omit the buttonhole, simply make a closure out of cloth or elastic cord. Or sew on snaps instead.*

# apron (or Layering Apparel)

I believe in beauty and functionality. It's wonderful when things in our life that inspire joy are also useful.

Like many, I wear an apron to protect my clothing when I create. Typically, I find myself wiping my hands on my apron, which might cause some to shudder; however, I feel that this only adds to the beauty and splendor of the apron, offering a glimpse into a moment in time that is forever imprinted on cloth. It is important not to be afraid to have fun in your apron—mess it up, create a story!

The multitude of buttonholes on this apron are not only design elements; they allow the wearer to choose the fit and the way in which the apron will be worn. This makes the garment artistic and functional as well as unique. This apron also can be worn as a layered piece of clothing.

Hand-dyed fabrics add so much depth and personality to your work. While dyeing appears time consuming, it is actually quite easy to do. A bit of boiled water and a splash of dye along with some salt (to help stabilize the color) create the perfect color bath. Simply dip your fabrics until you achieve your desired color and set aside to dry.

## GATHER THIS TO BEGIN

Buttons (varied)

Embellishments (optional)

Fabric: felt (wool or craft); muslin; shop towel (dyed terry)

Fabric dye (I used RIT in dark green and tan)

Ink: VersaCraft® or fabric ink (black)

Iron and ironing board

Needle (embroidery)

Pearl cotton #5 (or embroidery floss)

Pen: permanent or fabric pen

Pinking shears

Quilting machine needle, size 14/90

Quilting machine thread

Rubber stamps (background, text, alphabet)

Scissors

Sewing machine

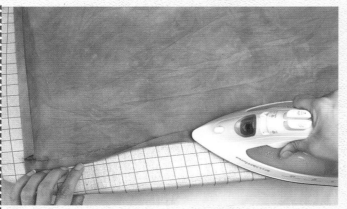

**1»** Cut a piece of muslin approximately 40" × 26" (102cm × 66cm). Dye the muslin and a terry shop cloth in the same batch (follow manufacturer's instructions). When the muslin is dry, iron it. Along 1 long side and the 2 short sides, turn each edge about ½" (13mm), and fold another ½" (13mm) and iron flat.

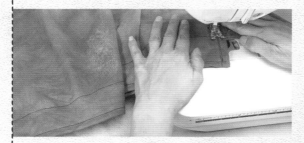

**2»** For the remaining long side, turn the edge once about 2" (5cm). This will be the top of the apron, with an exposed frayed edge as a design element. Sew a straight stitch around the bottom and 2 sides. Sew a straight stitch across the top and bottom of the top hem.

**3»** Add a decorative zigzag stitch around the sides and bottom.

**4»** Rip two 3" × 32" (8cm × 81cm) strips of stained muslin. Fold the first strip in half lengthwise and sew a line around the perimeter twice. Repeat for the other strip. With VersaCraft® ink, stamp both sides of each strip. (I like to use a different stamp for each side.) Stamp along the 2" (5cm) top hem as well.

**5»** At 1 end of each strip, sew a series of 6 or 7 buttonholes sized to the buttons you've chosen for the waistband.

**6»** Position about 5½" (14cm) of the other end of each strip to the top hem of the apron, aligning the edge of the strip with the side of the apron. Secure with a series of straight stitches. If you like, add embellishments such as the red felt heart as I've sewn here.

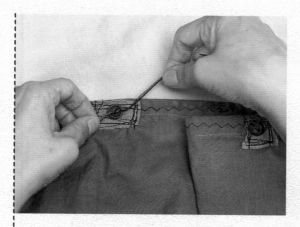

**7»** Along the bottom hem, add decorative elements such as scraps of dyed shop towel and buttons (see photo, left).

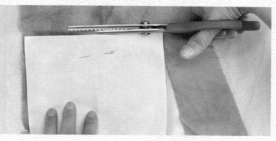

**8»** Use the pattern on page 119 to cut out a pocket from coffee-stained muslin. Trim the top of the pocket with pinking shears.

**9»** Stamp your favorite inspiring quote on the pocket with alphabet stamps. Add the attribution with a LePen™ by Marvy®.

**10»** If you like, add some hand-embroidered elements. I like to sew with more than 1 color of thread at a time. Here, I have added little stars. To make, stitch a cross, then bisect the corners of the cross with 2 straight stitches to form an X. I also added some French knots (see pages 104–105, Steps 21 and 22).

**11»** Machine-sew 3 or 4 rows of decorative stitching along the top of the pocket. Add any final details you like with the sewing machine, such as the red felt heart I added here. Then, sew the sides and bottom of the pocket to the apron.

**12»** Finally, stitch on embellishments where the buttons will go along the waistband, about 16" (41cm) from each side of the apron. Sew on the buttons to finish.

To wear, position the apron front, then wrap the ties all the way around the back to the opposite sides. Button the ties to the waistband according to the fit you want.

# art QUILT t-SHIRt

As a connoisseur of artful clothing, it occurred to me that I could and should be wearing my art. Soon thoughts of using my mini quilting methods in clothing started to formulate in my head. With stamp in hand, I set to work combining layers of muslin, organza and lace, layering and sewing, and stamping and playing all at the same time.

For this project I utilized the ombre dyeing technique, achieved by dyeing fabric at intervals, starting with one end and slowly moving to other end. The darkest color is the starting point with the first submersion of the fabric into the dye; the fabric is left in until a dark variation of the color is absorbed. This is followed by the second section, which is submerged for a much shorter period, creating a lighter shade. The final submersion creates the lightest shade. During each submersion, the previous color or colors remain in the bath.

For the quilt patch for this piece, start with a fabric base and layer and sew onto it. Keep in mind how the size of your quilt will look on your T-shirt. Fabric glue sticks are helpful when sewing small pieces together—pins tend to get in the way. Don't forget to embellish with hand embroidery or machine stitches. I like the look of a frayed edge and rip my fabric. If you prefer a cleaner look, iron fusible webbing to the back of your fabric. This will keep it from fraying.

Organza is a good top layer that can act as a sheer pocket for capturing small objects such as beads, buttons, tiny stones or shells. After you've sewn the pocket shut, stitch around each object to secure it between the layers. Explore the possibilities—what about small plastic toys or other objects that can't be sewn like buttons? (When choosing items, remember that your T-shirt will need to be washed.)

Have fun with all the little details. Try patterned fabrics or vintage handkerchiefs. Stitch a few scraps left over from your art quilt to the bottom hem, a sleeve or to the back of your T-shirt. This will add even more depth to your wearable artwork.

## GATHER THIS TO BEGIN

Bowl (for dyeing)

Buttons (varied)

Fabric: assorted scraps; cheesecloth; muslin; organza (sheer)

Fabric dye (I used RIT Dye in tan)

Ink: VersaCraft® or fabric ink (black)

Needle (embroidery)

Pearl cotton #5 or embroidery floss (for button ties)

Quilting machine needle, size 14/90

Quilting machine thread

Rubber stamps

Scissors

Sewing machine

T-shirt (cotton; white or light enough to take dye color)

Trim: lace

**1»** Mix up a batch of dye according to the package directions. Throw in your assorted scraps of muslin, cheesecloth, lace, etc. Dip just the bottom half of the shirt into the dye.

**2»** Lay the remaining part of the shirt over the side of the bowl to keep it up and out of the dye. Leave the bottom part of the shirt in the dye for several minutes. Hold it up to check the color.

**3»** When the bottom of the shirt is the color you want, immerse the center section into the dye bath for a few minutes to achieve the next layer of color. Finally, dip the top of the shirt into the dye to complete the final color layer.

Wring out all the other pieces you're dyeing at this time as well. Rinse everything according to the package directions and let dry.

**4»** To make the large front patch, cut 6" x 6" (15cm × 15cm) and 5" × 4" [13cm × 10cm] pieces of muslin. Using VersaCraft® Ink, stamp over both muslin pieces with a background stamp. Stamp an additional scrap of muslin to be used later.

Layer a piece of cheesecloth over the 6" x 6" (15cm × 15cm) stamped muslin. Then layer on the 5" × 4" (13cm × 10cm) muslin. Decide on other elements such as lace and word element patches.

**5»** When you are happy with your composition, sew the layers together. Start with the large muslin/cheesecloth/smaller muslin sandwich, then stitch on the lace and the word element. Also sew on any buttons you've chosen. Finally, sew the whole patch to the front of the T-shirt.

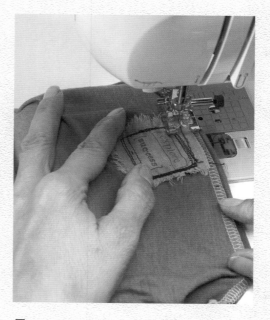

**6»** To create tags that will go on the inside and outside of the back of the neck, first stamp two 2" × 2" (5cm × 5cm) scraps of muslin with word stamps of your choice. Add decorative stitching to each.

**7»** Sew the tags simultaneously to the inner and outer back neck of the shirt with 1 running stitch around the smaller of the 2 pieces.

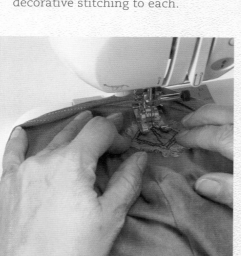

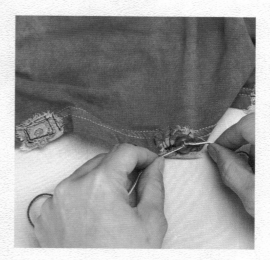

**8»** Sew a word element patch to 1 of the sleeves at the hem.

**9»** Finish with a series of small patches along the bottom hem and add a button or 2.

The task Thy wisdom hath assigned
Oh let me cheerfully fulfil;
In all my works Thy presence find,
And prove Thy good and perfect will.

# singed art

I cannot pinpoint the exact time that I started incorporating burning into my artwork. Nevertheless, I have found that by adding layers of burnt textiles, ribbons and embellishments, I expand my palette and my options.

Burning is definitely one of my favorite ways to alter fabric, resin papers and transparencies, and it's an extremely wonderful way to add a finished look to fabric artwork pieces. My preferred method is to mix wool felt with Kunin (acrylic/polyester blend) felt for the dramatic effect the two yield when combined.

Since I work primarily in my studio, this is where I burn pieces. I'm able to open a large utility door, which allows for a proper amount of ventilation. During inclement weather I take my burning activity indoors. I suggest that, if you have the opportunity, practice your burning techniques outdoors, with a mask. (See page 21 for more about my approach to burning.)

I promise you: Once you begin to add burnt layers to your artwork, you will be fascinated and quickly hooked. Singed art is the perfect way to explore the possibilities of heat-altering fabrics.

## GATHER THIS TO BEGIN

Decorative paper: assorted scraps

Embellishments (assorted)

Fabric: assorted scraps; organza

Metal tray, cookie sheet or other heat-resistant surface

Pearl cotton #5 (or embroidery floss)

Quilting machine needle, size 14/90

Quilting machine thread

Resin paper (scraps; see page 17)

Sewing machine

Spoon (metal)

Votive candle, heat gun or butane lighter

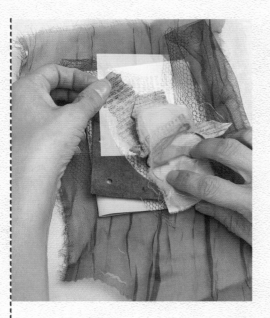

**1»** Gather scraps of paper, resin paper and assorted fabrics for layering. Play around with them to find a general composition that you like.

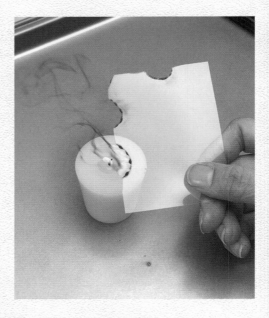

**2»** Burn the edges of some of the scraps with a candle, butane lighter or heat gun. (See more about these methods on page 21.)

**3»** Layer everything in a stack and machine stitch to secure.

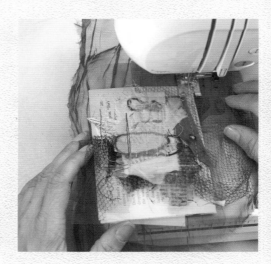

**4»** Continue to add elements; sew everything together until you feel it's all secure.

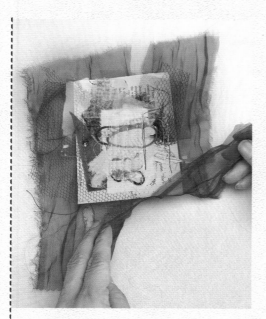

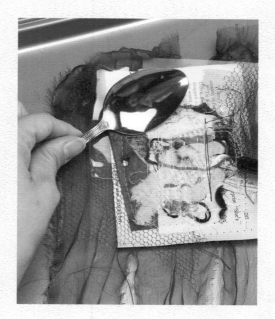

**5 »** Shred the organza so that it will shrink better.

**6 »** You might want to use a lighter to burn some sections. You can quickly extinguish smoldering areas with the bowl of a metal spoon.

**7 »** Use a heat gun to burn the rest of the piece.

## DISPLAYING SINGED ART

*The finished pieces can be hand stitched onto a gallery stretched canvas or placed within a shadow box or frame. Also, the pieces are the perfect size for incorporating into a larger piece of artwork.*

# SHELL FRAME

It's human nature to gather mementos. A shell or a twig quickly becomes a piece of history when added to our collection of memories. Photos of our shared times and adventures also accumulate quickly. This shell frame is a marriage of ideas: bits and baubles gathered long ago and a photo of my daughter when she was three years old. The result is a medley of recollections from the summer days of my daughter's childhood.

Fabric frames are a wonderful and adaptable medium. They can be taken so many different directions and are applicable to a broad range of creative ideas.

When preparing your frame, let your photo be the muse that guides you. Once you have found that perfect image, add elements that invoke memories related to the photo. This project provides the perfect opportunity to bring cherished souvenirs out of boxes and drawers to be enjoyed.

The process of layering is quite obvious in most of the projects in this book. Altering fabric by dyeing or scrunching it up in the dryer to add wrinkles produces an effect that alludes to history behind the piece. Once you begin working in this manner, you will find yourself looking deeper into your creative process. New discoveries will start to flow.

So, pick a favorite photo and create a frame around it! It's time to enjoy the memories you have made.

## GATHER THIS TO BEGIN

Beads (assorted, plus large bead for the wire frame stand)

Bowl (for dyeing with coffee)

Buttons (assorted)

Cotton batting (Warm and Natural)

Drill with 1/16" (2mm) bit

Fabric: cheesecloth; muslin; organza

Gel medium

Ink: StazOn® or fabric ink (saddle brown)

Instant coffee

Needle (embroidery)

Pearl cotton #5 (or embroidery floss)

Pen: LePen™ by Marvy® or fabric marker

Photo of choice (to fit vinyl pocket)

Pliers (chain nose, round nose)

Quilting machine needle, size 14/90

Quilting machine thread

Rubber stamp (background)

Sewing machine

Shells

Trim: lace

Vinyl (clear)

Wire (16-gauge) and cutter

**1»** Mix up at least 3 cups of strong instant coffee and pour it into a bowl. Soak the fabric that you are dyeing first in water. I like to dye several types of fabric, lace and cheesecloth all at once so I can use the extra pieces later. Wring out each piece and set it aside to dry.

**2»** Rip a coffee-dyed piece of muslin to 10½" × 9" (27cm x 23cm). Trim a piece of organza and 2 pieces of Warm and Natural cotton batting to the same size. Stamp over the surface of the muslin with a background stamp of your choice. Lay the stamped fabric over 1 piece of Warm and Natural, then arrange additional elements such as shells, buttons or pieces of lace. Also position your photo where you would like it to be.

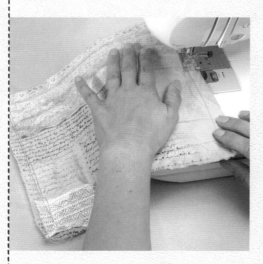

**3»** Keeping your layout in mind, begin sewing. Secure small elements like lace first, but run 1 line of stitching around the entire piece.

**4»** Cut a small square of organza. Place it where you want it to serve as a pocket for a shell or trinket, then sew 3 sides to the muslin. Slide in the shell or trinket. Sew the fourth side closed.

**5»** Cut a piece of clear vinyl a bit larger than your photo. Cut a piece of organza to cover as much of the remainder of the muslin piece as you would like. Layer the organza onto the muslin, then layer the vinyl on top. Secure both to the muslin by running a stitch around the sides and bottom of the vinyl. (Leave the top open to slide in your photo later.) This will be easiest if you use a larger straight stitch such as 5.0.

**6»** Divide the organza area into pockets by sewing lines through the organza and muslin to create squares. Fill the pockets with shells before sewing the pockets closed.

**7»** If you have shells that you do not want to put in a pocket, drill a hole in them with a 1/16" (2mm) bit.

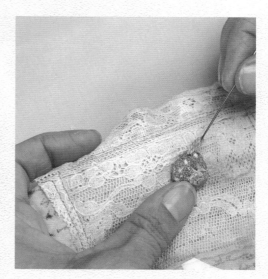

**8»** Next, sew the drilled shells like buttons to the muslin piece.

**9»** If you like, you can create a handwritten embellishment using a LePen™ by Marvy® or fabric pen on a scrap of muslin. Sew this piece on by hand using an embroidery needle and pearl cotton or embroidery floss.

**10»** On the remaining piece of Warm and Natural, stitch a decorative element in the center, like the flower I made here. Layer the stitched piece of Warm and Natural over the back of the front frame piece (the side with the vinyl pocket should be facing out). Sew the layers together by stitching 3 channels about ¼" (6mm) wide—1 along the top and 1 along each side.

**11»** Cut a 32" (81cm) length of 16-gauge wire and form a loop at 1 end. Hold the wire against the side of the frame and bend it to fit the side of the frame.

**12»** Thread a large bead onto the wire. Make a loop at the other end and bend the wire as you did in Step 11, creating an arc in the middle. Insert the straight sides of the wire into the 2 side channels you sewed in Step 10. Work the arch so it rests flat with the bead at the center when the frame is upright.

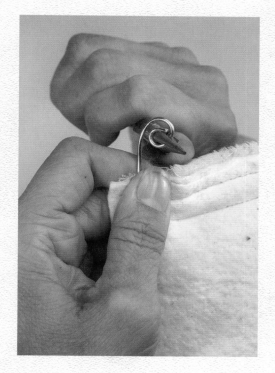

**13»** Cut a 14" (36cm) length of wire and coil it at 1 end. Poke a hole at 1 end of the top channel you sewed in Step 10. Push the uncoiled end of the wire through to the other side to create support for the top of the frame.

**14»** Coil that end of the wire, then center the wire in the top channel.

## HIDDEN TREASURE

*To add an extra (invisible) layer to your piece, place a brief poem or information about the photo within the layers of the frame. Although hidden, this piece of history will be treasure for whoever finds it in the future.*

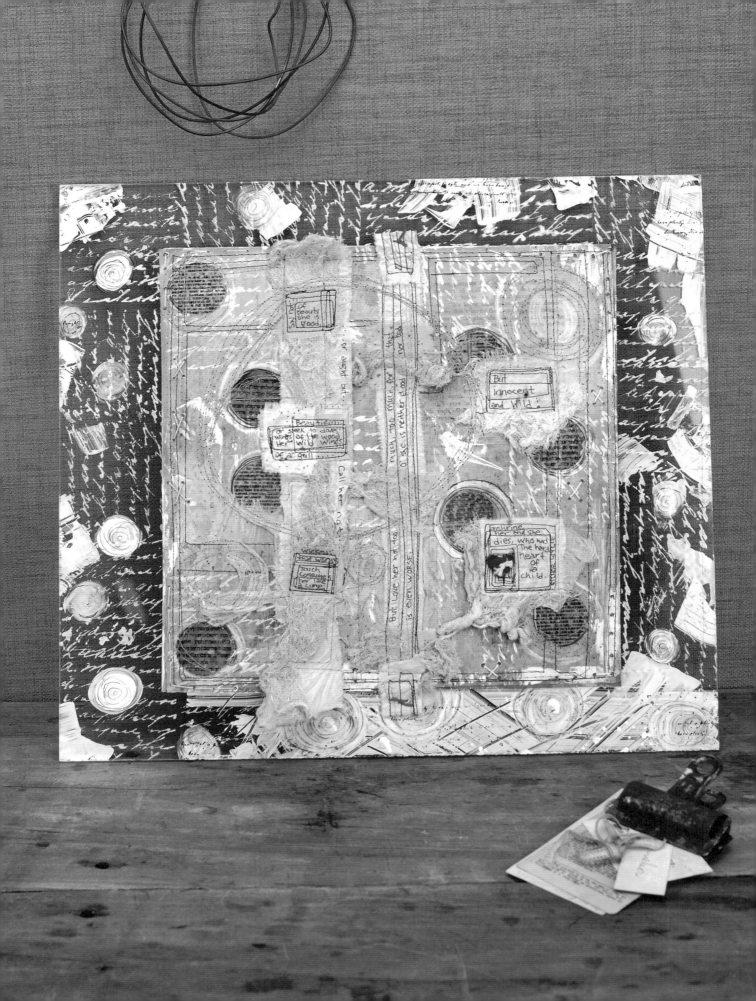

# PLEXIGLAS-FRAMED artwork

For the most part, my artwork is combined with meaningful words or quotes, and often a motto or poem inspires me to create a piece of art. (For instance, a poem called "Beauty," written 90 years ago by Elinor Wylie, is central to this project. I was captivated instantly by her haunting expressions, which resonated deeply like an ancient echo.) You, too, can make art using a long love poem or a mantra that is close to your heart.

I used Roc-lon® Roc-rol™ Multi-Purpose Cloth for the base of this project. It is an extremely versatile heavy fabric with a smooth finish that needs no priming, and it does not soak up paint. Also, it is wonderful to sew on. Heavy canvas is an acceptable substitute—just make sure that you add a layer of gesso to the surface beforehand.

Framing one's artwork remains a debate among artists; however, in this case the frame itself becomes an extension of the art. Plexiglas comes in many different sizes and thicknesses, which makes it ideal to work with.

Imagine all the projects you can create with plexiglas! A bit of thought, paint, fabric and fun is all you need.

## GATHER THIS TO BEGIN

Baby wipes

Brushes (wide bristle, foam)

Bumpon™ bumpers (clear)

Decorative paper: book text

Drill with 1/16" (2mm) bit

Fabric: muslin; Roc-lon® Roc-rol™ Multi-Purpose Cloth (or heavy canvas)

Flush cutters

Gel medium*

Gesso (black, white)*

Glaze (ivory)*

Ink: StazOn® (Blazing Red)

Leather punch

Needle (embroidery)

Palette knife

Paper punch

Pearl cotton #5 (or embroidery floss)

Pen: LePen™ by Marvy® or Pigma® Micron®

Pencils: graphite (black and white)

Plexiglas

Resin paper (see page 17)

Rubber stamps

Scissors

Sewing machine

Quilting machine needle, size 14/90

Quilting machine thread

Titan Buff Fluid Acrylic*

Wire (24-gauge)

*I prefer products by Golden Artist Colors.*

**1»** Apply a coat of black gesso over a piece of multipurpose fabric or heavy canvas. When dry, use gel medium to adhere book text to the cloth. Squeeze a bit of Titan Buff onto the paper and dry brush it over the text.

**2»** Brush a dab of black gesso loosely over the paper.

**3»** Smear it all with a baby wipe and remove most of the paint.

**4»** Squeeze out some ivory glaze and brush it over the entire surface.

**5»** Make random marks with a palette knife and white gesso.

**6»** Brush some white gesso over a background stamp.

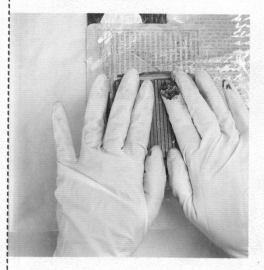

**7»** Stamp onto the surface in random spots. (Lift the stamp straight up to avoid smearing the gesso.)

**8»** Add a bit of color with an ink pad and a spatter stamp.

## WRITING ON FABRIC

*You can write on fabric with just about any pen. I suggest you practice on a variety of fabric scraps with different pens prior to working on your project. Some pens work, some bleed and some run out of ink quite quickly. One method I use is, prior to writing on fabric, I add a small amount of gesso to the fabric's surface. This gives it tooth and allows my pen to move freely.*

*When I'm not concerned about washability, my favorite pen is LePen™ by Marvy®. It comes in a rainbow of colors and has a fine nib that is perfect for writing on fabric. Graphite pencils are also fantastic for writing on different surfaces; they give great definition without detracting from your work.*

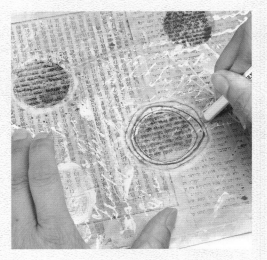

**9»** When the gesso is dry, add some resin paper shapes, like the circles I punched here using a craft paper punch. Usually I use gel medium to adhere them.

**10»** Doodle around the shapes with black and white graphite pencils.

**11»** Create any muslin fabric elements that you want in your collage (including handwritten quotes, such as the lines from "Beauty" that I've used here). Stitch them to the paper. Straight-stitch some decorative elements as well.

**12»** Measure your finished piece of artwork and add 2½" (6cm) all around. Cut a piece of acrylic glass to this measurement. (If you can't cut plexiglas yourself, order it cut to size.)

Using a palette knife, apply some Titan Buff and white gesso to the plexiglas. Stamp onto the surface with the same designs you used in the artwork. Add stamped areas on both the front and back of the plexiglas for increased depth. Finally, draw circles over some of the painted areas with a black graphite pencil.

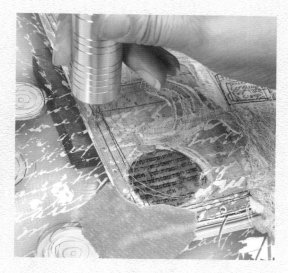

**13»** When the plexiglas is fully decorated and dry, find the center, then measure about 1" (3cm) down from where the top edge of the artwork will be positioned on the acrylic. From this point, measure about 2" (5cm) horizontally in both directions and mark. Drill a $1/16$" (2mm) hole at each of these 2 spots. Thread a length of wire (24-gauge is fine) through the 2 holes and twist to secure. This serves as a hanger.

**14»** Center the artwork over the plexiglas and secure it with light-tack or removable tape in the corners. Mark a series of holes around the edge of the artwork and drill a $1/16$" (2mm) hole at each spot. Holes can be placed creatively for the stitching you'll do in the next step.

## TIPS ON DRILLING PLEXIGLAS

~ *It is quite easy to drill through plexiglas; however, keep in mind that the drill will cause the acrylic to heat up and melt onto your bit if you slow your drilling speed. Once you drill down through plexiglas, pull your drill directly up and out. It's also important to drill onto a piece of scrap wood to protect your table surface.*

~ *While drilling, pay attention to the debris that comes out of the hole. If the debris starts to build up, stop and remove it from the hole or drill bit; otherwise, you might crack the acrylic by forcing the drill bit through the hole.*

**15»** Thread a needle with pearl cotton or embroidery floss and sew the artwork to the plexiglas through the drilled holes. Put 1 clear Bumpon™ bumper on the back of each of the 4 plexiglas corners to protect the artwork and the wall when the piece is hanging.

# "create" banner

Pennants and banners have roots that date back many centuries. Both, created with fabric, were used to display family lineage and announcements during celebrations and arrivals. In our world today, we see pennants and banners everywhere, from studios and creative spaces to parties and sports events.

A banner is the perfect project to personalize either for ourselves or as a gift to someone dear to us. A word that offers encouragement or a phrase that reminds us of why we do what we do, spelled out in a banner, is a wonderful addition to a wall or passageway.

The simple construction of a banner makes it very appealing. Paper, fabric, ribbons, embellishments and other baubles and trinkets turn a basic piece of artwork into a treasure. We can integrate a time-honored tradition into our daily lives with a little time and materials.

## GATHER THIS TO BEGIN

Alphabet letters
(ready-made, with glitter)

Beads, pearls and crystals

Craft paint

Decorative paper: such as
sheet music

Doves, small plastic (available
in the wedding section of most
craft stores)

Drill with 1/16" (2mm) bit

Fabric: cheesecloth; felt; lace;
muslin; organza

Fabric dye

Flush cutter

Ink: StazOn® or fabric ink
(timber brown and saddle brown)

Leather punch

Needle (embroidery)

Paper towels

Pearl cotton #5
(or embroidery floss)

Plastic cup

Pliers (chain nose, round nose)

Quilting machine needle,
size 14/90

Quilting machine thread

Rubber stamps (deeply etched)

Scissors

Sewing machine

Wire (24-gauge, any color)

Yarn or other fiber (fuzzy)

**1»** Squirt a dollop of craft paint into a small plastic cup. Dilute it with about ½ cup (118ml) of water. Stir, then dip in a dry paper towel.

**2»** Squeeze the excess water from the paper towel and set it aside to dry (or iron it). At the same time, dye various scraps of fabric or cheesecloth that you may want to use, too.

Cut out six 4" × 6" (10cm × 15cm) pieces of felt. Create the individual letter pennants in whatever order you like. Start by placing 1 piece of felt over a sheet of decorative paper (such as sheet music); tear the paper to leave a border around the felt.

**3»** Lay out elements to decide how you want the pennant to look. If you wish, stamp on a scrap of muslin to act as a little patch. Trim or tear the elements to size and layer.

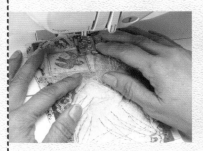

**4»** Secure the layers (including the muslin patch) to the felt and background paper with free-form decorative stitching.

**5»** After layering, sew the letter onto the pennant with a double strand of embroidery thread; simply tack it down in a few places by bringing the thread over the letter (see photo above).

**6»** Move on to the next letter pennant. If you plan to use several stamped elements on 1 pennant, it makes sense to stamp them all at once so they are ready to go.

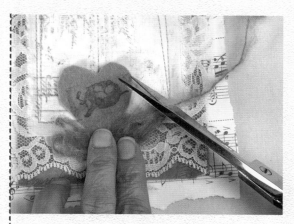

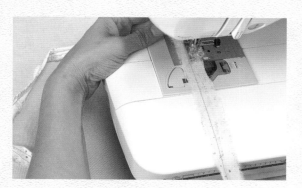

**7»** Again, layer the fabric elements for this pennant the way you want them to look. Secure the majority of them with the sewing machine. (Hand-stitching some elements adds additional texture.)

Here, I am creating a fiber "nest" for my little heart element. If you'd like to try this, cut several lengths of fuzzy yarn.

**8»** Secure the heart (or other element that goes in the nest) first. Arrange the yarn around the heart and stitch back and forth over it to secure it.

**9»** Stamp on 1 side of a piece of muslin; on the other side, spatter paint or use a spatter stamp. To create ties for the pennant, tear the muslin into long strips about 1" (3cm) wide. Sew around the perimeter of each strip.

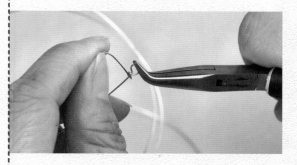

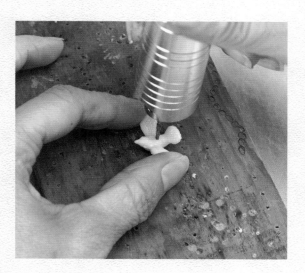

**10»** I like to have little dangles hanging from a couple of pennants for added interest, such as this small nest: Start with 36" (91cm) of 24-gauge wire. About 2" (5cm) from 1 end, form a small loop with round nose pliers. Grasp the loop with chain nose pliers and wrap the tail of the wire around the base of the loop.

**11»** Drill a hole through 1 of the plastic doves using a ¹/₁₆" (2mm) drill bit.

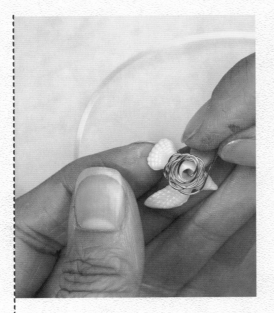

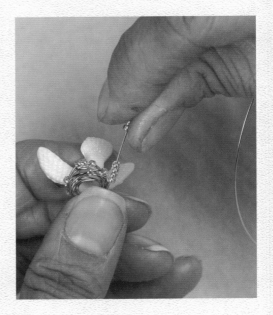

**12»** Thread the dove onto the wire so that the eye loop is on top of the dove. Bend the wire down flat against the dove's bottom and secure it with your thumb. Coil the wire to form a base for the nest.

**13»** Thread about 20 seed beads onto the wire. Coil the wire some more, working in the beads as you go.

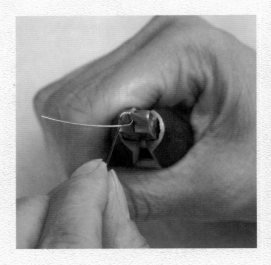

**14»** When the nest is as full as you want it, coil the wire back up the nest and trim it close against the bottom of the dove. Tie a piece of fuzzy yarn between the bottom of the dove and the nest.

**15»** Cut a 3" (8cm) length of 24-gauge wire. Using round nose pliers, create a small loop about ¾" (19mm) from 1 end.

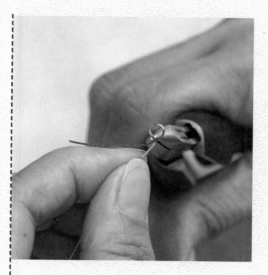

**16»** Where the wire starts to cross itself, grasp it inside the loop with chain nose pliers. Bend the loop up to center it over the wire.

**17»** Grasping the loop flat with chain nose pliers, wrap the tail of the wire around the base of the loop about 3 times.

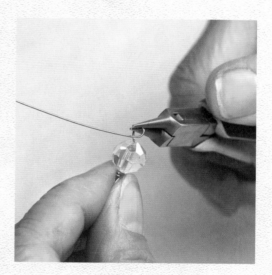

**18»** Trim the excess wire.

**19»** Thread a bead or crystal onto the wire. Bend the wire down 90 degrees. Near the hole of the bead, form another loop with the round nose pliers.

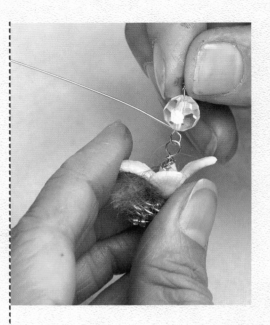

**20»** Thread the loop of the bead or crystal onto the dangler. (Here, I am linking it to the bird-nest charm.)

**21»** Again, grasp the loop flat with chain nose pliers and wrap the remaining wire around the base of the bead. Trim any excess.

**22»** For added interest, try stamping on the surface of the beads you'll use for the danglers. Here, I am stamping a variety of beads using a text stamp and StazOn® ink.

**23»** To create your own head pin, start with about 4" (10cm) of wire. Use the tip of round nose pliers to create a loop, then coil the loop a couple of times.

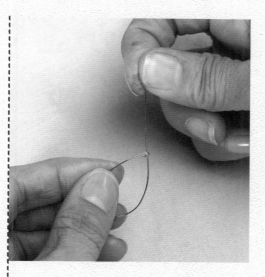

**24»** Thread the other end of the wire through the loop.

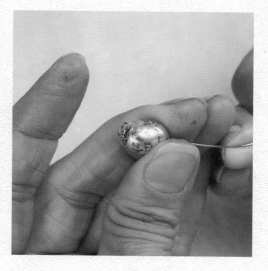

**25»** Pull the wire taut to create a knot at the end. I find it easier to tighten the knot by pushing a bead against it while tugging the wire.

**26»** Create a wrapped loop at the other end of the bead. Continue adding rosary-wrapped beads until the dangle is the length you want. (See page 103 for instructions on rosary-wrapping beads.)

**27»** Cut the stamped/spattered muslin strips into lengths about 14" (36cm) long. Punch holes at the top corners of the letter pennants. Tie the pennants together with the muslin strips, threading dangles onto the strips between some of the pennant cards.

# tree wall art

I often integrate wire into my fabric art as a way to attach small items or beads. When I came up with the idea to create this tree, the wire somehow ended up taking center stage!

I also often embed "secret journaling" in my work by using handwritten or book text that holds special meaning to me. The text becomes a backdrop as only parts are revealed in the process of burning the tree trunk and leaves.

The combination of Kunin felt and organza with paper and cotton thread gives these leaves a true-to-life appearance. You'll find that using synthetic fabrics alongside natural fabrics or heat-resistant papers will generate all kinds of new ideas.

Because of the fumes emitted, do your burning outdoors or next to an open window. You can take further precaution by wearing a ventilation mask. (There's more on using heat to alter fabric on page 21.)

(There's more on using heat to alter fabric on page 21.)

## GATHER THIS TO BEGIN

Beads or pearls

Bookbinder's awl

Butane lighter

Decorative paper: book text or handwritten journal page

Dowel

Fabric: duck cloth (coffee-stained); felt (brown Kunin); muslin; polyester organza; tulle

Fiberfill

Heat gun

Ink: StazOn® or fabric ink

Metal tray, cookie sheet or other heat-resistant surface

Needle (embroidery)

Pearl cotton #5 (or embroidery floss)

Pen: LePen™ by Marvy® or fabric pen

Perfect Pearls™ Pigment Kits (Ranger)

Pliers (chain nose and round nose)

Quilting machine needle, size 14/90

Quilting machine thread

Rubber stamps

Scissors

Seam ripper

Sewing machine

Sponge daubers (I used Tsukineko daubers)

Spoon (metal)

Wire (24-gauge [I used annealed steel]) and cutters

**1»** Start with two 9" × 12" (23cm × 30cm) pieces of brown Kunin felt. Between the pieces of felt, layer a couple of pieces of tulle, 1 piece of organza and 1–2 pieces of book text (enough to cover the surface of the trunk). The book text should be at the bottom of the layers over the piece of felt.

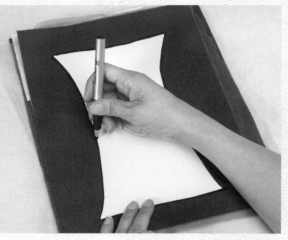

**2»** Photocopy the trunk pattern (see page 120), cut it out and place it over the felt sandwich. Trace around the pattern with a pen.

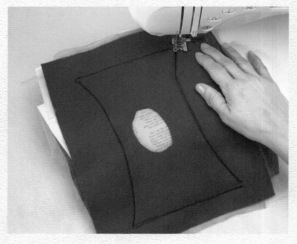

**3»** Cut a hole in the center of the trunk, then machine sew around the traced outline to secure the sandwich together.

**4»** Cut out the trunk shape about ¼" (6mm) outside of the sewn line.

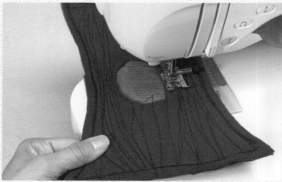

**5»** Stitch lines to emulate the texture of bark up and down the trunk. Sew around the perimeter of the hole as well.

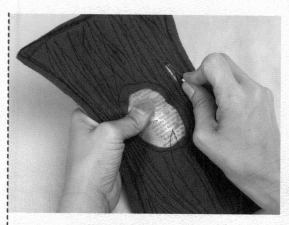

**6»** When you are happy with the bark stitching, use a seam ripper to cut through the hole to reveal a cross secton of fabric layers. Don't cut through the book text. Also cut some vertical slits through some of the stitches in the bark.

**7»** Using a heat gun, burn through the layers of fabric in the areas you cut with the seam ripper. Also burn the outside edges of the trunk. When finished, set the trunk aside.

**8»** To create leaves, start with a 9" × 12" (23cm × 30cm) piece of green Kunin felt. Add 1 layer of book text and 1 layer of green organza. Pin the layers together, then machine sew a variety of free-form leaf shapes. Sew vein lines as well. I like to sew around the perimeter of the leaves a couple of times to make them more stable.

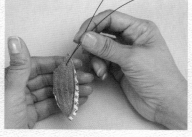

**9»** Cut the individual leaves out with scissors. Use a heat gun to burn the edges of each leaf, which will make them curl a bit.

**10»** Cut three 14" (36cm) lengths of wire. Use an awl to make a hole in the end of 1 leaf, then thread 1 piece of wire through the hole. Fold the wire approximately in half.

**11»** Snugly wrap 1 end of the wire a couple of times around the other end near the bottom of the leaf.

The number of leaves you create is up to you, but I made about 30 leaves for this tree.

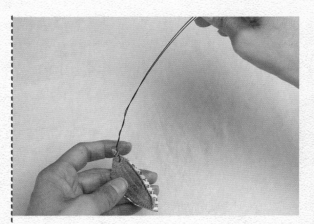

**12»** Loosely wrap the wire along the other half of the wire.

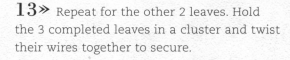

**13»** Repeat for the other 2 leaves. Hold the 3 completed leaves in a cluster and twist their wires together to secure.

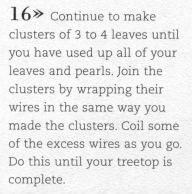

**14»** Stamp the pearl beads with a text stamp and StazOn® ink. Cut one 6" (15cm) length of 24-gauge steel wire, make a knot on 1 end and thread on a pearl. Repeat with another 6" (15cm) length of wire and a second pearl.

Add each pearl to the leaf cluster by first wrapping its wire around the main stem of the cluster. Next, wrap the wire around the base of the pearl, then again around the cluster's stem. Repeat for the second pearl.

**15»** Curl the excess ends of the pearl wires by coiling them around an awl.

**16»** Continue to make clusters of 3 to 4 leaves until you have used up all of your leaves and pearls. Join the clusters by wrapping their wires in the same way you made the clusters. Coil some of the excess wires as you go. Do this until your treetop is complete.

**17»** Cut 4 matching un-stamped muslin squares. Stamp a bird image on 2 of the squares and stack them on the plain squares. Sew around the perimeter of each bird, leaving a small opening. Add decorative stitches for the birds' talons, then stuff the birds with fiberfill.

**18»** Hand sew the birds closed, then cut each one out about ⅛" (3mm) beyond the stitched outline. Color the birds using a sponge dauber and 2 colors of blue or teal ink.

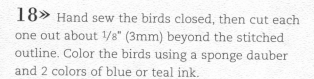

**19»** Use a dauber to color a section of plain muslin. Fold the muslin in half and machine stitch a wing shape in the same way you stitched the leaf shapes. Cut out the wing and hand stitch it to a bird's body.

Repeat the process for the second bird, but sew the wing on the opposite side of the body so the wing shows when the bird faces the other direction.

**20»** Cut a 4" × 20" (10cm × 56cm) piece of coffee-stained duck cloth. Burn the edges of the cloth with a lighter. When an edge smolders, extinguish it with a spoon.

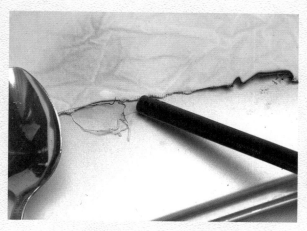

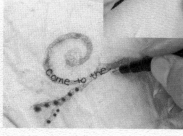

**21»** Stamp patterns along the bottom of the cloth with Perfect Pearls™, then apply the pearl powder over the tacky area with a soft brush. Use a couple of colors at once, if you like. Tap off the excess powder before brushing a second color over the design.

**22»** With a pen, add details such as writing or dots. Repeat this process until the entire bottom section is decorated

Fold the top over about 1½" (4cm). Machine stitch across the bottom of the folded cloth to form a sleeve for a dowel.

**23»** Assemble everything. Machine sew within the perimeter of the trunk all the way around to secure it to the duck cloth. Hand stitch the branches and leaves at the top of the trunk, then hand stitch the birds into place. You can add other elements, such as a nest.

Hang the finished piece using a dowel or old-fashioned clamp hanger. Even if you use a hanger, insert a dowel through the sleeve to keep the top stiff.

# "brave heart" WALL HANGING

The poetry of E. E. Cummings speaks to me. I adore his unmistakable style and lines that oftentimes deal with themes of love and nature. I wrapped this interactive hanging heart around his poem, "i carry your heart with me." I envisioned Cummings' words in every aspect of the design. As I created this piece, it became a virtual fabric journey. Layers upon layers of both seen and unseen beauty dance with one another in this fabric piece. This is my ode to E.E. Cummings.

I label my tortured hearts as "Brave." Our hearts are, figuratively and literally, our life lines. We feel them breaking when we are let down and filled with joy when something extraordinary occurs. The heart form is a constant in my art.

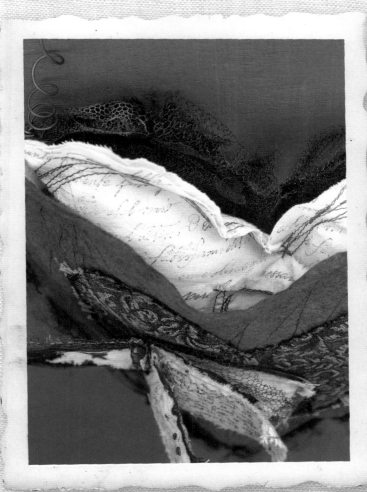

## GATHER THIS TO BEGIN

Beads (assorted)

Bleach pen (Clorox® Bleach Pen® Gel or liquid bleach)

Book text or handwritten journal page

Bookbinder's awl

Dowel (½" [13mm] diameter)

Fabric: felt in black and red (Kunin craft felt only; no wool); cotton jacquard; muslin; polyester organza; tulle

Fiberfill

Heat gun

Ink: StazOn® or fabric ink

Leather punch

Letter punch set and hammer (optional)

Metal sheet (24-gauge, any kind) for heart charm

Metal tray, cookie sheet or other heat-resistant surface

Needle (embroidery)

Quilting machine needle, size 14/90

Quilting machine thread

Pearl cotton #5 (or embroidery floss)

Pen: LePen™ by Marvy® or fabric pen

Pinking shears (optional)

Pins

Pliers (round nose, chain nose)

Ribbon (I used vintage seam binding)

Rubber stamps

Scissors

Seam ripper

Sewing machine

Spoon (metal)

Tea light candle

Tin snips

Vinyl (clear)

Wire (16-gauge [I used annealed steel] and 24-gauge) and cutters

**1»** Cut a large black felt heart to the size you desire, then cut a second, smaller heart. Apply a bleach pen to both black hearts (or use regular bleach in a bowl, diluted with water).

When you are satisfied with the bleaching effects, rinse the hearts thoroughly in warm water.

**2»** Cut 2 pieces of red craft felt to a heart shape that is slightly smaller than the large black heart. Add decorative machine stitching with black thread to each piece. (I prefer to stitch a line around the perimeter of the shape first, then fill the space in with zig-zag lines.)

## WORKING WITH BLEACH

*Bleaching may be the easiest surface-altering technique that I use. Ordinary household bleach is effective on such natural fibers as cotton, linen, rayon, broadcloth, denim, piqué, gauze, velveteen, corduroy and jacquard. If the fabric contains polyester, which is usually color-fast, the color may not discharge.*

*You can also brush or drip the fabric with bleach. A bleach pen will yield a more controlled look, and patterning is easier to achieve. Removing the top layers of dye will reveal an array of colors. Commercial fabrics are dyed in multiple applications with a broad variety of under colors, so results will be different each time you employ this method.*

**3»** Cut 3 random holes through 1 of the red heart pieces. Singe the holes over a tea light candle to open them up (blow the flame out before it gets too big). Cut a small wedge out of the heart's center, using pinking shears to create jagged edges.

**4»** For each hole, cut a few small scraps of a variety of fabrics, layer them together and sew each stack of layers to the front of the heart over a hole, stitching around each one.

**5»** Use a seam ripper to open the center of the holes and use scissors to remove some of the fabric. Also use scissors to snip the layers to make them ruffle a bit around each hole.

**6»** Use a heat gun to burn the edges of the layered fabrics a bit. The organza shrinks up quickly.

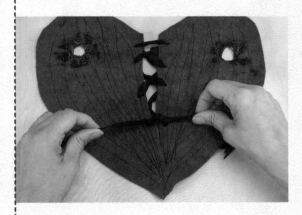

**7»** Use a ¼" (6mm) leather punch to make 5 holes down each side of the wedge on the front of the heart. Working from the top down, insert both ends of a length of black ribbon or strip of fabric through the 2 top holes from front to back; adjust to make sure both halves of the ribbon are equal.

Continue to lace the wedge from front to back. Do not pull the ribbon too taut; the gap at the top of the wedge should remain visible. At the bottom, tie the ribbon into a bow.

## THE EFFECTS OF BURNING

*A few years ago I started burning felt to achieve a distressed effect. I suggest that you experiment a bit with burning (see pages 21 and 69), as it takes some time to discover the various effects you can produce from this form of fabric manipulation.*

**8»** Place the larger of the 2 bleached black hearts under the red heart with the holes. Position a scrap of clear vinyl under each of the holes, sandwiched between the red and black hearts. Pin each piece of vinyl in place on the black heart.

**9»** Sew 3 sides of each piece of vinyl to create pockets, which are sewn to the black heart but show through the holes in the red heart. Decide what you want to show inside each of the holes. Here, I have used some found text, tiny pearls and a heart crystal.

Stuff your selected items into the pockets. Sew the fourth side of each pocket closed.

**10»** Cut 2 tulle hearts and 1 organza heart about 1½" (4cm) larger all around than the red hearts. Sew the smaller bleached heart onto the front of the second red heart. Make a sandwich with the red hearts on the outside and the tulle and organza hearts in the middle. Pin everything together.

To secure the layers, sew around the perimeter of the heart, leaving the top of the heart open. Use scissors to snip through the tulle/organza about every 1½" (4cm) around the heart. Burn the layers a bit with the heat gun.

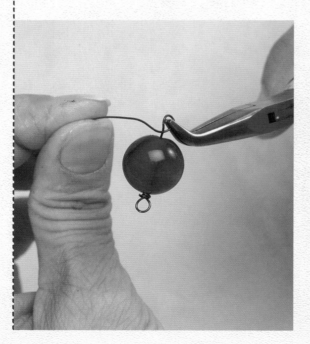

**11»** Create a stuffed muslin insert for the red heart. Cut out 2 muslin hearts that are about 1" (3cm) smaller all around than the finished red heart. Stamp over the surface of each muslin heart with a text or background stamp.

Cut a small piece of coffee-stained muslin for a pocket and stamp a heart in the center of it. Sew it to 1 of the muslin hearts along 3 sides. Sew the 2 muslin hearts together, leaving about a 3" (8cm) opening. Stuff the heart with fiberfill, then sew it closed.

To make an enclosure for the pocket, create a small strand of wire-wrapped beads. Rosary-wrap the first bead and repeat for as many beads as you like, linking them as you go.

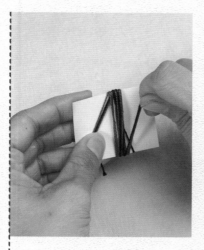  

**12»** Cut three 1-yard (1m) strands of pearl cotton or embroidery floss. (Mix different colors, if you like.) Wrap them as a group around a card 1½" (4cm) wide.

**13»** Carefully remove the wrapped bundle from the card.

**14»** Wrap a 2" (5cm) length of pearl cotton or floss around the top of the bundle about ¼" (6mm) from the top. Tie a snug knot to secure it.

**15»** With scissors, cut the loops of the bundle opposite the knot. Trim the ends of the strands to clean them up and make them even in length.
    Attach the completed tassle to 1 end of the strand of rosary-wrapped beads.

## HOW TO ROSARY-WRAP A BEAD

*Begin with a 3" (8cm) length of 24-gauge wire. Using round nose pliers, make a loop about 1" (3cm) from one end of the wire. Wrap the tail of the wire around the base of the loop. Thread on a bead, then create a loop in the wire at the other end of the bead and wrap the tail of the wire around that loop.*

*    To link, insert the unlooped wire of a bead through the finished loop of a second bead. Make a loop on the wire of the first bead and wrap the tail of the wire around the base of the loop.*

**16»** For the other end of the bead strand, create a charm from a piece of 24-gauge metal sheet. Use tin snips to cut a heart shape. If you wish, use letter stamps to spell out a message on the heart.

**17»** To create a small fabric book, rip coffee-stained muslin into four 2½" × 7" (6cm × 18cm) pieces. Layer scraps of organza and tulle between the first 2 pieces of muslin. Sew down the center (spine) of the muslin page spread to secure the layers.

**18»** Next, sew around the perimeter of each page on each side of the spread.

**19»** Repeat for the other spread. Sew the 2 spreads together down the spine. If you like, you can singe the tulle around the edges a bit.

Now you're ready to decorate your pages. I like to use a combination of embroidery stitches and journaling with a Marvy® LePen™.

**20»** French knots are a fun element to add. To make one, start with a double strand of embroidery floss. Wrap the floss around your needle about 5 times.

**21»** Push the needle back through the fabric near where the thread came out of the fabric, pulling the floss through the wrapped portion on the needle. (Be sure not to sew through the muslin page on the other side; try to begin and end your stitch between layers.)

**22»** After your pages are decorated the way you want, attach the book to the center of the small black heart by hand stitching down the center of the book.

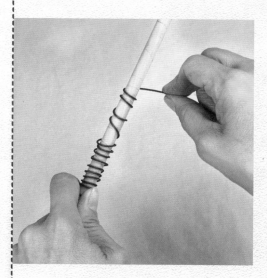

**23»** Cut a 1-yard (91cm) length of 16-gauge steel wire. Leaving a 3" (8cm) tail, wrap the wire around a ½" (13mm) dowel until 3" (8cm) remain at the other end.

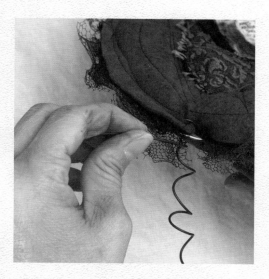

**24»** Ease the coil off the dowel and stretch it out a bit. Use a leather punch to make holes on either side of the red heart positioned about ½" (13mm) from the edge near where the heart's opposite sides meet.

Create an eye at 1 end of the wire with round nose pliers. Thread the wire through 1 hole in the heart, then wrap the excess around the base of the loop. Repeat for the wire's other end and the other hole.

# Close the Language Door HANGING

*Close the language-door,*
*and open the love-window*

    ~ RUMI

Doors are universal symbols. Most of us see doors only as architectural passageways between the indoors and outdoors and between rooms. I like to ponder the larger symbolism of doors.

For centuries doors have stirred our imaginations. The Masters often painted doors into their artwork as symbols of mysteries to "unlock." Guarding or receiving keys to a door is significant; being granted passage is often due to heroic or symbolic growth. No wonder doors appear in literature and the arts representing change. Opening a door admits ventilation and light, but a shut door may change the physical atmosphere of a space by enclosing it. Doors intrigue us with questions of what lies beyond.

The "language of love" doors in this project are full of promises and mysteries, with little ideas and trinkets tucked here and there. Let the door be your guide when creating your own expression of language.

## GATHER THIS TO BEGIN

- Beads (assorted in shades of blue)
- Bowl (for dyeing)
- 4 buttons
- Copper sheet (36-gauge foil)
- Cotton batting (Warm and Natural)
- Craft paint (seafoam green)
- Decorative paper: book text or hand-written journal page
- Dowel (³/₈" [10mm] in diameter)
- Drill with ¹/₁₆" (2mm) bit
- Fabrics: Kunin felt (navy); muslin; polyester organza (navy, seafoam green); tulle
- Fiberfill
- Heat gun
- Ink: StazOn® or fabric ink
- Kosher salt
- Leather punch or bookbinder's awl
- Letter punch set with bench block, hammer
- Liver of sulfur
- Needle (embroidery)
- Pearl cotton #5 (or embroidery floss) in variegated brown and cream or white
- Pen: LePen™ by Marvy® or similar
- Pencil
- Pliers (chain nose, round nose)
- Quilting machine needle, size 14/90
- Quilting machine thread (cream, aubergine)
- Rubber stamp (deeply etched script)
- Saw (for trimming sticks to size)
- Scissors
- Sewing machine
- Silk ribbon (for tying on bead pendants)
- Spray bottle with water
- Sticks (small)
- Straight pins
- Straightedge
- Trim: lace and other fabric trim
- Wire (24-gauge) and cutters

**1»** Dilute about 4 tablespoons (15ml) of acrylic paint in about 2 cups (473ml) of water. Dunk a 12½" × 19½" (32cm × 50cm) piece of muslin in the diluted paint to dye it. (Also dye various elements, such as lace and cheescloth, as desired.)

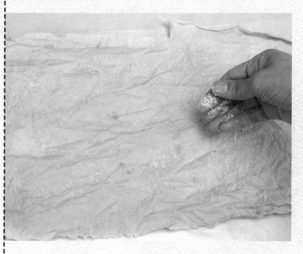

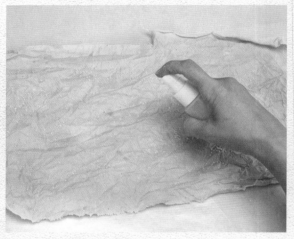

**2»** Wring out the fabric, spread it out, then sprinkle kosher salt over the entire surface.

**3»** Spray the salted areas with water. Set the piece aside for a bit.

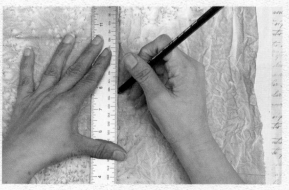

**4»** Cut a 12½" × 19½" (32cm × 50cm) piece of cotton batting and a 13½" × 20½" (34cm × 52cm) piece of muslin. Stamp the muslin around the perimeter with a script stamp. Layer the batting over the stamped muslin, then layer the dyed fabric on top. Pin the layers to secure.

**5»** Sketch a cathedral door onto the dyed muslin.

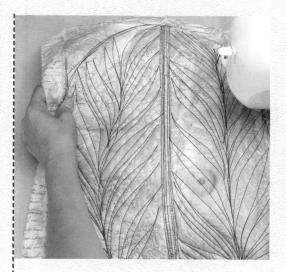

**6»** Stitch around the doors and fill them in with decorative stitching. Sew straight lines down the center to divide the doors. Leave about a ¼" (6mm) space between them to cut down the center.

**7»** Use scissors to cut down the center between the doors. Also cut around the curve at the top of the doors. (Don't cut down the straight, outer portion—the hinges—of the doors.)

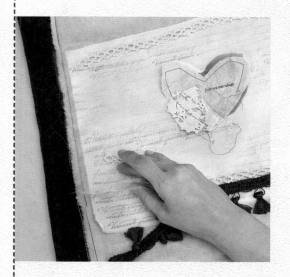

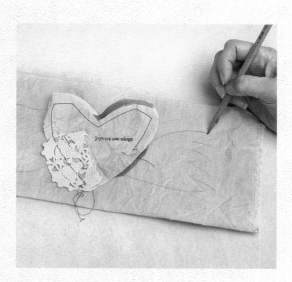

**8»** Cut two 14½" × 23½" (37cm x 60cm) pieces of navy felt. (This double layer provides stability for the artwork.) The pieces can be rectangular; or extend the top into a half circle shape for a crown. (See photo on page 106.) Cut a muslin piece just smaller than the felt and layer it beneath the felt as a backing.

Design what you want to go behind the doors. Here, I use a larger dyed muslin piece as a base, then stamped muslin under a layer of organza as a "stage" for my focal element, a dyed-muslin heart. I also use lace and pompom trim. Sew down all layers and trim.

**9»** If you'd like to add wings to your heart element, place the heart on a piece of muslin. Sketch in wings on either side of the heart.

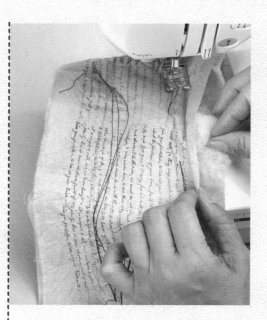

**10**» Stamp over the sketched muslin with a script stamp, then add another layer of muslin and machine stitch both pieces together, leaving a small opening at the top. Stuff the wings lightly with fiberfill, then sew closed.

**11**» Cut out the wings, trimming close to the stitching lines.

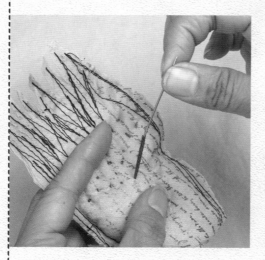

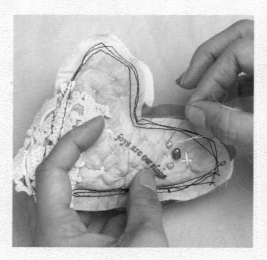

**12**» If you like, add hand quilting to the stuffed wing and heart elements. Knot a length of pearl cotton or embroidery floss. Insert the needle through the bottom of the element, pulling the thread through, then push the needle back in very close to where the needle emerged. Repeat over the surface as you'd like to give the work a tufted look.

**13**» Add pearls or beads in the same way, although you may need to use a beading needle for this.

**14»** Think about the elements you want for the panels on the front of the doors. If you'd like to include a long poem in the door panels, divide the poem into 4 stanzas. Cut 4 tag shapes from a piece of 36-gauge metal sheet. (Copper is used here.)

**15»** Using a hammer, bench block and letter punch set, stamp each of the 4 segments of the poem onto the 4 metal tags.

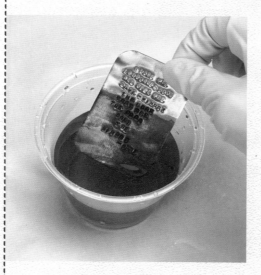

**16»** Dip each metal tag in liver of sulphur to blacken it, then set all 4 aside to dry.

**17»** Lay out the 4" (70cm) panels on the door fronts, choosing the fabric elements and trims you want to use in addition to the metal tags.

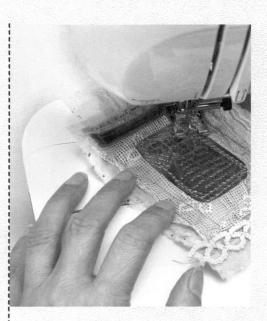

**18»** Stitch the layered fabric panels together. When the fabric elements are complete, sew on the metal tags by machine using the quilting machine needle, size 14/90. Hand stitch any final elements, such as beads or sticks, onto each panel as well.

**19»** Lay out the panels so the poem segments read in order, 2 panels per door. Secure each panel to the door by stitching up 3 sides, adding fiberfill stuffing, then closing the final side.

**20»** Use the doors layer as a guide to position your focal element correctly on the back layer. Machine stitch the element to secure it.

**21»** Sew each door to the back layer by stitching up and down the "hinges" several times.

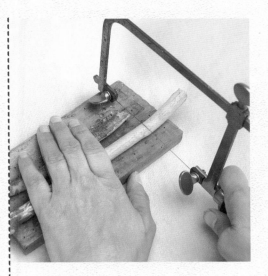

**22»** To create door handles, saw 2 heavy sticks to the same length.

**23»** Using a ¹/₁₆" (2mm) bit, drill holes through both ends of each stick. Drill 2 more holes in the center of each stick evenly spaced between the ends.

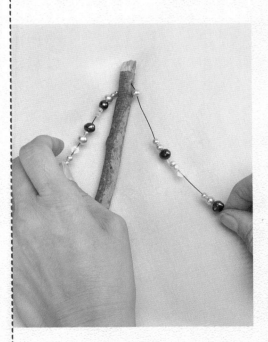

**24»** Cut a 36" (91m) length of 24-gauge wire. Guide it through the hole at 1 end of a stick. Center the wire so it's divided evenly. Thread assorted pearls, beads and crystals onto both halves of the wire.

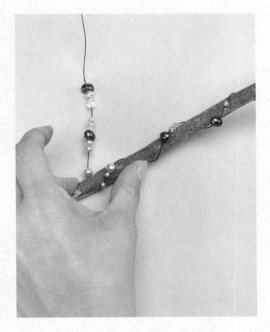

**25»** Wrap the wire up the length of the stick, spreading the beads as you go. Pass the wire through the hole at the other end of the stick.

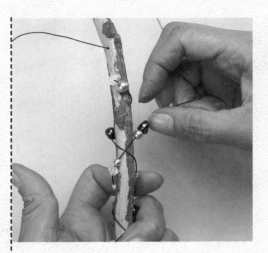

**26»** Wrap in the other direction, creating a crisscross pattern up the stick. Pass the end of the wire through the first hole from the opposite side.

Thread pearls, beads and crystals on the second half of the wire and move back down, then up the stick in the same crisscross fashion, inserting the wire through the hole at the other end of the stick as you go.

**27»** Twist both wire ends together to secure; trim the excess. Use chain nose pliers to create crimps in the wire. Repeat Steps 24–27 with the second stick to complete the pair of door handles.

**28»** Finish off the piece with decorative hand stitching and additional decorative trim at the top of the door. For door closures, punch 2 matching holes near the top and bottom edges of the doors with a leather punch.

**29»** Cut 2 small pointed sticks. Wrap wire strung with beads around 1 end of each. These sticks, inserted through the holes as indicated in the photo, will hold the doors shut when the piece is hung.

## FINISHING TOUCHES

~ *Use a heat gun to create rolled edges on the navy felt. (Do this carefully.)*

~ *Embroider the navy felt edges of the piece with French knots and cross stitches.*

~ *For beaded elements for the door panels, make small beaded pendants and tie the tops with silk ribbon. Stitch through the ribbon to secure the pendants onto each panel.*

~ *On the interior layer, embroider the top and bottom sections of the background muslin with French knots in variegated brown pearl cotton or embroidery floss.*

~ *Sew a dowel to the top back of the piece with cream or white pearl cotton or embroidery floss. Stitch through all three layers of felt and muslin, ceating large cross stitches on the front of the piece as you sew the dowel into place so the stitches blend in with the other embroidery.*

**30»** Sew on the door handles by positioning a button so it lies beneath the top middle hole on a stick. Using pearl cotton or embroidery floss, insert the needle through 1 hole of the button (leave a 2" [5cm] tail), through the door, then through the hole in the stick. Thread on a bead, then guide the needle back through the same hole in the stick and through the door and another hole in the button. Cut the thread, then securely tie the ends and trim.

**31»** Repeat with another button for the lower middle hole on the same stick. Repeat the entire process with 2 more buttons on the stick handle for the other door.

## A CROWN FOR YOUR DOOR

*The project door crown was created with a vintage pearl collar and part of a beaded bracelet. If you do not have access to these types of pieces, hand sew pearls or beads onto your background. Other options include lace collars, clip-on earrings, broken pieces of jewelry or elaborate decorative trim, which can be hand stitched down*

# patterns

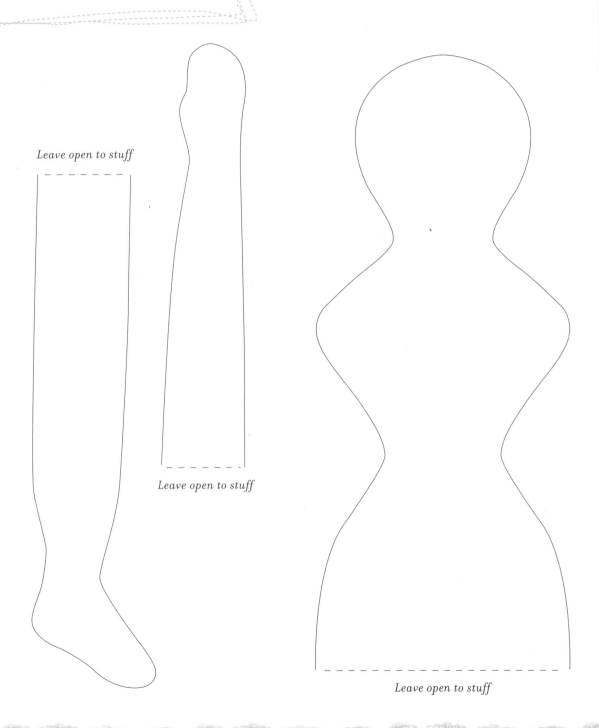

*Leave open to stuff*

*Leave open to stuff*

*Leave open to stuff*

*art girl doll* PATTERN (PAGE 22)
ENLARGE TO 133%.

APRON FOR *art girl doll*
ENLARGE TO 111%.

DRESS FOR *art girl doll*
(*Pattern is full size*)

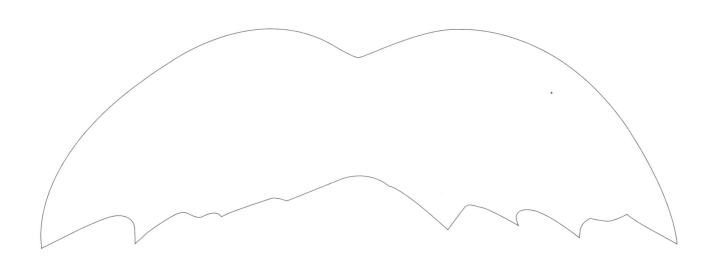

WINGS TEMPLATE FOR *art girl doll* OR DOLL CLOTHES (OPTIONAL)
ENLARGE TO 120%.

POCKET PATTERN
FOR *apron*
(*or layering apparel*)
ENLARGE TO 182%.

TREE TRUNK PATTERN FOR *tree wall art*
ENLARGE TO 116%.

# resources

DMC USA
www.dmc-usa.com/
*(embroidery floss and pearl cotton)*

Coats & Clark
www.coatsandclark.com
*(sewing and quilting thread as well as other fibers)*

Environmental Technology Inc.
www.eti-usa.com
*(Envirotex Lite resin)*

Green Pepper Press
(Michelle Ward)
http://greenpepperpress.com/
*(maker of some of the stamps used for projects in this book)*

Kelly Paper
www.kellypaper.com
*(paper products cut to order)*

The Kunin® Group
www.kuningroup.com
*(felts and fabrics)*

Marvy® /Uchida of America, Corp.
www.marvy.com
*(LePen™ plus other pens, tools and supplies)*

Quilting Arts
www.quiltingarts.com
*(Ruth Rae DVDs)*

Ranger
http://rangerink.com/
*(ink, Grungeboard, Perfect Pearls™ Pigment Kits)*

Red Lead Paper Works
www.redleadpaperworks.com
*(maker of some of the stamps used for projects in this book)*

Rit Dye
www.ritydye.com
*(fabric dye information and projects)*

Roc-Lon®
www.roc-lon.com
*(muslins and Roc-rol™ Multi-Purpose Cloth)*

Ruth Rae
www.RuthRae.com
*(artwork and inspirational works)*

Stampington
www.stampington.com
*(maker of some of the stamps used for projects in this book)*

Tsukineko
www.tsukineko.com
*(inks, markers and sponge daubers)*

United State Plastic Corp.
www.usplastic.com
*(Plexiglas)*

Volcano Arts
www.volcanoarts.biz
*(online source for hard-to-find tools and materials like the Japanese screw punch, mica, liver of sulphur, waxed linen, bookbinder's awls and sheet metal saws)*

PERVENCHE
PREMIER AMOUR

MYOSOTIS
NE M'OUBLIEZ PAS

let your soul delight itself

with fervent heart and soul

Thou art

our hope, we glorify

Thy grace.

words bring life and

light to the soul.

divine the secrets of Thy

memories filled their hearts.

Sing joyfully

water the earth, and make it bring forth and bud

Thou art the strength of our life

O Thou who knowest the secrets of the heart,

Thy lovingkindness never ceases.

Thy hand, for our souls

Truth eternal and unchanging

Eternal truth

Thou shalt love

courage

Trustfully I confide

helpfulness.

Thy grace and goodness

with all thy soul

heart

knowledge.

from the hand

Create in me a clean heart

gratefully

everlasting

IRIS
ÉLOQUENCE

COQUELICOT
REPOS

COME UNTO HIM.

nd ye shall find rest.

I believe I gave my heart to you

beloved

*Viola May Perdue.*

my soul shall be

what lies *within*

we are, in some ways, all teachers

*I* *know not how to answer.* I love you.

r love above all else."

o you have a sweetheart whom you love?"

in-to your souls.

mutual passion

I loved you always,

I devote myself,
—with all their powers

and spirit.

"Once bit, twice shy,"

# about
# Ruth

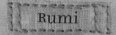

"*let the* BEAUTY *of what you* LOVE *be what you do.*"

Rumi

RuthRae

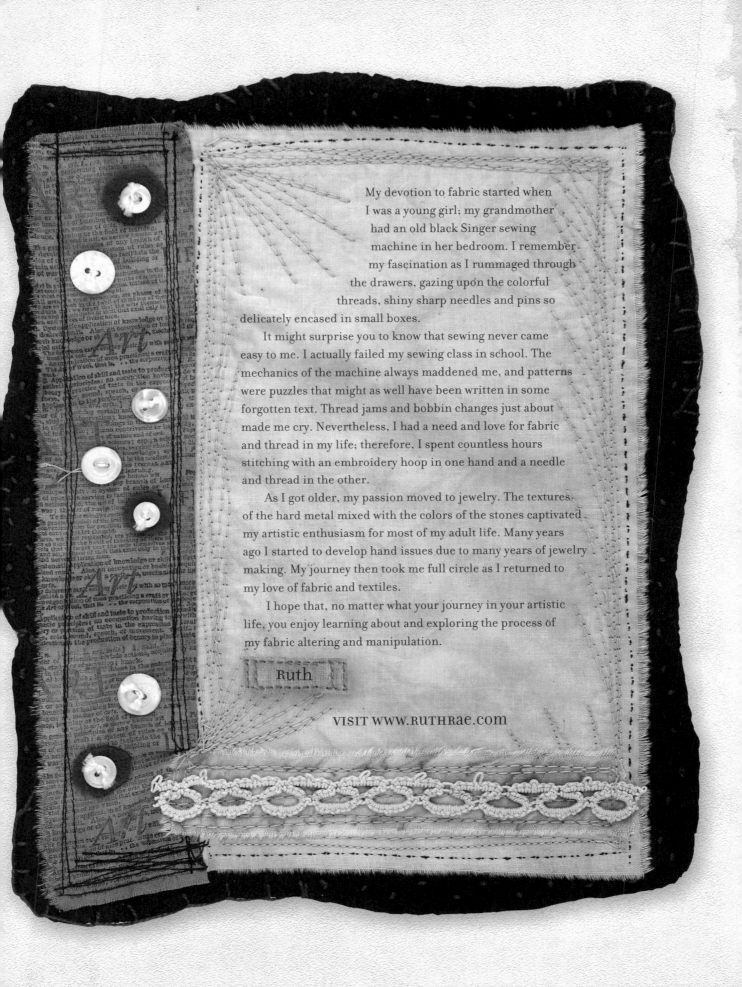

My devotion to fabric started when I was a young girl; my grandmother had an old black Singer sewing machine in her bedroom. I remember my fascination as I rummaged through the drawers, gazing upon the colorful threads, shiny sharp needles and pins so delicately encased in small boxes.

It might surprise you to know that sewing never came easy to me. I actually failed my sewing class in school. The mechanics of the machine always maddened me, and patterns were puzzles that might as well have been written in some forgotten text. Thread jams and bobbin changes just about made me cry. Nevertheless, I had a need and love for fabric and thread in my life; therefore, I spent countless hours stitching with an embroidery hoop in one hand and a needle and thread in the other.

As I got older, my passion moved to jewelry. The textures of the hard metal mixed with the colors of the stones captivated my artistic enthusiasm for most of my adult life. Many years ago I started to develop hand issues due to many years of jewelry making. My journey then took me full circle as I returned to my love of fabric and textiles.

I hope that, no matter what your journey in your artistic life, you enjoy learning about and exploring the process of my fabric altering and manipulation.

Ruth

VISIT WWW.RUTHRAE.COM

# index

# INDULGE YOUR CREATIVE SIDE
## WITH THESE OTHER F+W MEDIA TITLES

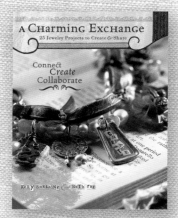

## A CHARMING EXCHANGE

*Kelly Snelling and Ruth Rae*

Inside *A Charming Exchange* you'll find the works and words of more than 30 artists with an array of varying creative styles and insights on collaborative art. Learn how to create 25 jewelry projects using a wide variety of techniques, from working with basic jewelry findings, beads and wire to incorporating mixed-media elements such as solder, fabric and found objects into charms and other jewelry projects. The book even offers ideas, inspiration and resources for you to start your own online swaps and collaborations.

ISBN-10: 1-60061-051-X
ISBN-13: 978-1-60061-051-6
paperback
128 pages
Z1653

## PRETTY LITTLE FELTS

*Julie Collings*

Inside this playful book, you'll find more than 30 projects to tickle your fancy. *Pretty Little Felts* shows you how to combine all kinds of felt with unexpected mixed-media materials, including vintage fabric, paper, glitter, metal, beads, ribbon and wire. From useful pouches and needle books to delicate jewelry and whimsical ornaments and doodads, there's something here for every crafter. All the projects are simply made with basic sewing and papercrafting techniques. A helpful "getting started" section gives information on dyeing and stitching felt, as well as specific instructions for deconstructing wool clothing.

ISBN-10: 1-60061-090-0
ISBN-13: 978-1-60061-090-5
paperback
128 pages
Z1979

## TAKING FLIGHT

*Kelly Rae Roberts*

In *Taking Flight*, you'll find overflowing inspiration, complete with a kindred spirit, in author and mixed-media artist Kelly Rae Roberts. Join her on a fearless journey into the heart of creativity as you test your wings and learn to find the sacred in the ordinary, honor your memories, speak your truth and wrap yourself in the arms of community. Along the way you'll be inspired by step-by-step techniques, thought-provoking prompts and quotes, and plenty of eye candy—pages and pages of the author's endearing artwork, along with a variety of works from her contributors.

ISBN-10: 1-60061-082-X
ISBN-13: 978-1-60061-082-0
paperback · 128 pages · Z1930

Join a world of crafters at
## www.mycraftivitystore.com
*Connect. Create. Explore.*